OFFSHORE INVESTMENTS *That* SAFEGUARD *Your* CASH

OFFSHORE

INVESTMENTS *That*

SAFEGUARD

Your CASH

ERIKA NOLAN
SHANNON CROUCH

The Sovereign Society

New York   Chicago   San Francisco   Lisbon   London
Madrid   Mexico City   Milan   New Delhi
San Juan   Seoul   Singapore   Sydney   Toronto

1 2 3 4 5 6 7 8 9 0   FGR/FGR   0 1 0 0 9 8

ISBN   978-0-07-162114-4
MHID 0-07-162114-8

Printed and bound by Quebecor World.

This publication is designed to provide accurate and authoritative information in regard to the subject matter covered. It is sold with the understanding that neither the author nor the publisher is engaged in rendering legal, accounting, or other professional service. If legal advice or other expert assistance is required, the services of a competent professional person should be sought.

> —*From a Declaration of Principles jointly adopted by a*
> *Committee of the American Bar Association*
> *and a Committee of Publishers*

McGraw-Hill books are available at special quantity discounts to use as premiums and sales promotions, or for use in corporate training programs. To contact a representative, please visit the Contact Us pages at www.mh professional.com.

CONTENTS

ACKNOWLEDGMENTS

We would like to express our sincere thanks to the following people for their help with this book:

Robert Kephart, Robert Bauman, John Pugsley, Bill Bonner, and Mark Ford for their philosophical beliefs and for their vision that gave birth to The Sovereign Society so many years ago. Their mentorship and support gave us the passion, the opportunity and the experience to write this book.

To all of the seasoned international professionals (and friends) Eric Roseman, Larry Grossman, Marc Sola, Colin Bowen, Robert Vrijhof, Thomas Fischer, Michael Chatzky, Mark Nestmann to whom we will always be grateful for sharing their honest viewpoints, and their secrets.

The team at McGraw-Hill for their patience and their belief that offshore solutions do work for the average investor.

To all of The Sovereign Society members we have met over the years at events around the world for sharing their successes, failures and their perspectives on wealth. Your desires and first-hand experiences have helped us refine the solutions offered within these pages.

And, last but not least, we would like to thank our families, friends and co-workers for their undying support of this project (and of us).

FOREWORD

GOING OFFSHORE: THE ONLY WAY TO GO

The first thing that should be said to someone who is thinking of "going offshore" is that it is like going into major surgery. The outcomes can differ enormously, depending on the skill of the surgeons and what they are trying to accomplish.

You may simply want to protect your money from volatility that comes with market crisis, economic instability, and a turbulent U.S. dollar. Or maybe you'd like to participate in investment opportunities in other parts of the world. Like a little nip and tuck, it's easy and relatively safe to do these things. Or you may want to try to protect your wealth from frivolous lawsuits—a more complicated and riskier procedure. You can do some major cost cutting on your taxes, too, but that could be an even more troublesome operation.

Whatever you're trying to do, you can be sure that other people have done it before you—including many of the richest and shrewdest investors in the world. The bad news is that a few of them never got up from the operating table. But that's why it's important to decide what you're trying to accomplish and make sure you have the right people working on it.

The second thing that should be said is that people in offshore destinations are likely to think and act very differently from the people you're used to dealing with at home. What's more, because of their odd accents and strange manners, it will be harder for you to size them up. Who's competent and who isn't? Who's honest and who isn't? You won't have a familiar frame of reference to help you sort them out. Of course, that's why you go offshore in the first place: you want something different. Still, you may be surprised at how different it is.

And the third thing to remember is that, if you are an American, federal laws may apply.

We take up that last point like strange meat in a cheap foreign restaurant, aware that it puts a lot of people off. The basic principle is that U.S. citizens are taxed by the U.S. government no matter where they are, almost just as if they lived in the United States. Not only that, but U.S. tax law applies to how they organize their affairs as well, not just the actual tax amount. Whether you are setting up a trust in Jersey or operating a business in East Timor, U.S. tax law may make a difference in what you do. That's why, as long as you remain a U.S. citizen, you must get advisors who are familiar with U.S. tax law.

A lawyer in Europe may tell you not to worry, for example. "There's no tax on that transaction," he says cheerfully. But even if there is no tax locally, it doesn't mean that there is no tax in the United States of America. Or, a trust company may put together a trust that is just what you want, unaware that it will be regarded as a sham transaction in the United States.

The reach of American law and the American tax process is so long and so grasping that some people decide to stop being American citizens. Recently, the U.S. embassy in London was so clogged with people trying to give up their citizenship that there was a six-month waiting list. Among the people who were renouncing their U.S. citizenship was the mayor of London himself, Boris Johnson, who was born in New York City in 1964.

Like many Americans abroad, Mr. Johnson had spent little time in the United States; his British parents just happened to be living there when he was born. A friend of ours from Switzerland, also born in the United States, left the country as a child; he barely speaks English, and he has visited only once or twice in the last 30 years. Still, he's required to file and pay U.S. federal taxes.

How does the typical European, African, or Asian deal with this obligation? "I just don't say anything," says our friend. And here we return to one of the key things you must realize: foreigners think differently. We Americans believe in paying our taxes and being straightforward with both our government and our fellow citizens. But many people overseas wouldn't dream of it. In some cultures, people tell you only what they think you want to hear. In others, they won't tell you anything.

"Only a fool files an honest tax return," say the French.

Living in France for 10 years, we turned to two sorts of professionals to help us with our local, French taxes. First, we worked with expensive American law firms in Paris. Later, we worked with local French accountants. The U.S. law firms—even when they were staffed with Frenchmen—always insisted that we diligently and earnestly figure out every detail, document every transaction, and make sure we were fully compliant with the letter of French law. However, the local accountants had a much different idea of what the law was—and how we should comply with it.

For example, France has a wealth tax that requires you to declare all your assets, wherever they are, and pay taxes on them. Among our assets at the time was a farm, 20 minutes outside Washington, D.C.

"How much is that worth?" asked the accountant.

"Oh, probably about $1 million," we answered.

"Wait . . . it's a farm, right?"

"Yes."

"How much farm income does it produce? How much revenue from it shows up on your U.S. tax declaration?"

"None—it's more of a hobby farm."

"Well, if it doesn't produce any revenue, it's not worth anything. You don't have to put that down. No French person would mention it."

"Oh."

The attitude toward truth is often different, as is the relationship between citizen and government. Many people regard their governments as an enemy or a predator. They see their goal as being to hide from it, to dodge it, and to mislead it. Very civilized, in our opinion.

But keep in mind that these are the same people who could be handling your account, your trust, or your estate!

Still, in our view, going offshore is the only way to go. Otherwise, you have no choice; you have to accept whatever your government and your economy give you. And that would be too bad, because every dog has its day. And while the United States was the hound to bet on for most of the twentieth century, the lead dog in the twenty-first century is likely to wag his tail to a Brazilian beat or favor sweet and sour puppy chow. In many emerging markets, economic growth rates are three times higher than those in the United States. China will have the world's largest economy in just 10 years. And wages are going up nearly 10 percent per year in India.

There are also the considerable financial advantages of traditional tax havens. Low taxes, financial security, solid currencies, secrecy—these countries offer services that you can't get in the United States at any price. There is a reason, for example, that many of the world's richest people favor Switzerland. It's one thing to make a fortune; it's quite another to hold onto it. The Swiss are experts at it.

And finally, there is simply the enchantment and adventure of going offshore. Even if we never made a dime out of it, we've enjoyed our rambles in the Swiss Alps, our eye-opening visits to Hong Kong and Bermuda, and our long summer evenings in Douglas, in the Isle of Man. No, it's not always cheap. And it's not always easy. But it's always the way to go.

Bill Bonner
President and Founder of Agora Publishing Inc.

INTRODUCTION

ELIMINATE THREATS TO YOUR WEALTH, WHILE SAFELY GROWING YOUR NET WORTH WITH COMPLETE PEACE OF MIND

Offshore investments and wealth strategies are highly effective and surprisingly affordable—however up until now, you may have heard very little or nothing at all about the opportunities that are available to you. And, it's the lack of quality information about offshore opportunities that keep most people from taking advantage of some of the world's best long-standing asset protection and investment opportunities.

In this book, we will reveal dozens of elite wealth strategies in easy to understand terms. We want to help you make informed decisions about your best financial options—how to secure everything you own once and for all against wealth predators and to protect your investment portfolio from the ravages of bear markets and superficial financial advice. You're not likely to learn about these techniques from the business section of your newspaper, on the financial news, or from local financial advisors. You won't learn about private offshore bank accounts—or about Swiss annuities that provide income and asset protection, or any of a many other asset protection solutions that we'll teach you about in this book. By the same token, there is a world of exceptional investment opportunities that are almost completely ignored by the mainstream press and Wall Street. We'll tell you about some of these in this book—including investments that have historically outperformed U.S. stocks for decades, yet are effectively censored by Wall Street and Washington.

You picked up this book for a reason. In fact, the odds are that there are many reasons why you did. Perhaps you want to put your estate in order once and for all. Or maybe you are looking for investment diversification in the wake of the unprecedented chain of devastating financial events which have unfolded in the past months. You may be seeking ways to maximize the savings in your retirement plan or looking to defer some taxes where appropriate. Perhaps you're looking for ways to diversify outside of the U.S. dollar, seeking a more global portfolio. Whatever your reason for joining us, we have the answers you're looking for. As the old saying goes, "If it's worth doing, it's worth doing well." And we couldn't agree more. *Offshore Investments That Safeguard Your Cash* offers you a path to true financial freedom and enjoyment of greater profits. Hundreds of thousands have successfully followed these strategies, and *so can you.*

Remember, however, that to complete this journey successfully, it's important that you do not skip steps or take shortcuts. If you invest your time properly and make the necessary effort, we promise that you'll reap the rewards. Do pay diligent attention and take notes. Underline or highlight important concepts, and write notes in the margins if you wish. After all, this is a learning experience, and you'll want to make the most of it.

THE FIRST STEP IS TO ASK YOURSELF: WHAT ARE MY FINANCIAL GOALS?

Think about this question, and take the time to define your goals clearly. No doubt you have personal goals—investments, privacy, retirement, and so on—or else you wouldn't be reading this book. But, you must decide on specifically what you want to accomplish.

Before you begin, take a moment to write down your goals. Don't worry about first impressions; just jot down your random thoughts. Ask yourself: "What are my objectives?" "What made me pick up this book?" "What keeps me up at night?" Be honest with yourself. Be realistic. You can always revise this list as you progress through the book. You can also engage in wishful thinking, which we encourage.

Next, prioritize these goals. Which is most important to you? Is it investment growth or asset protection? Currency diversification or finding a second home? Estate planning or privacy? Your honest answers to these questions will help you target the ideas and solutions presented in this book that are most appropriate for you. You may need only one solution, or you may discover several solutions or a combination of solutions (and there are many) that will meet your specific needs. Everyone is different when it comes to finances. One solution never fits all—we don't believe in "cookie-cutter" strategies here.

Lacking ideas? How about these?

- Are you worried about protecting your assets and avoiding claims?

- Are you having trouble with difficult business associates or dealing with the threat of lawsuits, or perhaps your spouse and children are unhappy and ungrateful?

- Is it just about making money? Is your main goal to increase the value of your investments, to grow your assets?

- Does the lack of financial and personal privacy in your home country bother you?

- Like most folks, have you been putting off creating a formal estate plan for your spouse and heirs, one that will guarantee their secure future should anything happen to you?

- Are you worried that you won't have enough money for your retirement?

Once you've set your targets, you can pick and choose the strategies in this book that make the most sense for you. You can do one of two things: select a few solutions to research further and put them in place gradually over time, or take one giant leap and devise a grand master plan.

The wonderful thing is that regardless of what you eventually choose to do, you're absolutely free to make changes as you learn. Revising your initial plans as you gain more knowledge and insight is perfectly normal. But don't fly blind. You will definitely need your very own tailored financial road map—a road map that accurately defines how you'll handle your financial affairs. Roll up your sleeves and do the hard work now. Later on, you can tear and compare—or scrap and change ideas from your first list, trading the old for the new as soon as you become comfortable with the offshore basics.

CHAPTER 1

WHERE IN THE WORLD IS "OFFSHORE"?

Offshore isn't just a place to swim, surf, or sail your boat . . . it's much more. For our purposes, offshore is everywhere *but* your home country. And specifically, when we talk about offshore in this book, we are referring to any place in the world that is *not* your home country and in which more advantageous financial and tax opportunities exist.

Over the years, a few nations have figured it out. These countries have set up legal systems so that they would stand out as money magnets and achieve the truly desirable status of "offshore financial havens." These financial centers are known as cash protectors and money generators for the world. They cater to foreign folks and foreign cash by enforcing strict laws guaranteeing privacy, asset protection, business development, access to global investments, and, in some cases, little or no taxes.

A few countries are known (and envied) for their international reputation. The most notable of these is Switzerland. In fact, the

World Bank estimates that more than half of the world's personal wealth—over $50 trillion—is stashed in about 60 or so asset and tax havens worldwide—Panama, Hong Kong, and so on. The lion's share of this personal wealth, however, is in Switzerland, with fully one-third of all offshore wealth comfortably secure in the country's bank vaults.

> Certain U.S. states, like Florida, New Hampshire, Alaska, and Texas, offer their citizens an escape from state income taxes. Offshore tax havens perform the same function for foreigners.

THE SMART STRUCTURE OF OFFSHORE CENTERS

We have visited most of these havens, and we can tell you from personal experience that the people who live there are ordinary folks just like us. They're folks who have the simple desire to make money and protect wealth in a more private and time-tested way.

These offshore locations play it smart. Their laws on investments are less restrictive and they place a premium on financial privacy. In these places, it's a crime to reveal a person's financial information. This is in stark contrast to the laws of the United States where it would be a crime NOT to reveal such information. But, there is more to most of these countries. The countries have their own laws and their own legal systems. This means that judges in these offshore havens restrict the ways in which foreign-based lawyers can practice in their court and how they can argue or plead a U.S. court claim or claims from any other nation. They oblige a foreign lawyer to start from scratch and establish proof again—in their jurisdiction. Small wonder, then, that so many U.S. lawyers hesitate or refuse to take cases involving defendants who have their cash and assets secured offshore. They recognize the difficulties—indeed, the impossibility—of gaining access to these offshore assets.

Offshore havens attract foreigners (and their money) because these havens still offer tax and financial advantages that have disappeared from the United States and are also nonexistent in other high-tax nations. It's a shame, because we remember clearly when America was created on the same low-tax, free-market, and entrepreneurial ideas—components that are making the current offshore havens so valuable.

Make the Most of the Benefits

Offshore havens offer opportunities that are not available to you in your home jurisdiction, such as:

- Asset protection that is more robust than what your American safe-deposit box offers (covered in Chapter 3)

- A wider selection of investments that can be much more profitable than what you'll find at home (covered in Chapter 4)

- Estate planning that is smarter and more efficient than what your local lawyer can set up (discussed in Chapter 5)

- Taxes that are significantly lower than what Washington demands (detailed in Chapter 6)

- Business regulations that are less cumbersome and thus promote entrepreneurship (covered in Chapter 8)

- Dual citizenship and a second passport that can be added conveniences (available in a few tax havens) (found in the book's Conclusion)

The beauty of offshore investing is that you don't have to pack your bags and move to enjoy most of these benefits. The only elements you need to move are your cash, your company, your retirement plan, and your other assets. This way, you can continue to enjoy your current lifestyle at home while your money enjoys better safety, security, and diversification abroad.

Offshore means more profits and more freedom! Here are five reasons to move your assets offshore:

- *More investment opportunities.* Because of U.S. red tape and rules, most of the world's leading investment and money managers will not do business with U.S. citizens or residents directly. By going offshore, you can gain access to these restricted investments. Only about 2,000 foreign securities are traded on U.S. markets, but there are many thousands of more profitable investments available offshore. This is explained in Chapter 4.

- *Currency diversification.* Investors who want to protect their portfolios can protect their wealth by creating a diversified currency portfolio which could include the Japanese yen, Swiss franc or the euro.

- *Safety and security.* Going offshore now is probably the most important investment decision confronting investors. That's because global banking diversification has never been more important with more than $1 trillion in write-downs tied to mortgage-backed securities and credit derivatives. European private banks, unlike money-center banks and commercial banks in the United States and elsewhere are far stronger and generally don't make mortgage loans or leveraged loans. These banks generate their revenues from wealth management, not gambling in derivatives. Despite the ongoing global turmoil, not a single Swiss bank has failed over the last 12 months.

- *Asset protection.* Lawsuits are an incurable epidemic in the United States. If a creditor obtains a judgment against you in the state in which you live, the judgment is easily enforced. However, if you invest or place your assets in a suitable jurisdiction like Switzerland, you can be nearly judgment-proof.

- *Financial privacy.* We all want protection from the prying eyes of business partners, estranged family members, or identity thieves. Simply put, assets that you place offshore are off the domestic asset tracking "radar screen" and protected by ironclad privacy rules that no longer exist in the United States.

IS GOING OFFSHORE LEGAL?

You are now familiar with the myriad benefits of going offshore—asset protection, tax minimization, investment opportunities, and much more. We are aware of how valuable these benefits may be to you. We would also like to banish any doubts you may have about using offshore strategies. No matter how much or how often we speak about the advantages of going offshore, the same question always pops up: "It all sounds good, but is it *really* legal?"

This question has come about because of a series of planned, unjustified attacks on offshore financial activity over the years by the U.S. Internal Revenue Service, the U.K. Customs and Revenue, Canada Revenue, and tax collectors in other high-tax nations. Needless to say, this has sowed confusion and fear in the minds of people who have shied away from offshore. It looks as if the tax collectors got what they wanted.

Yes, there are definitely U.S. reporting requirements and U.S. tax laws that you need to comply with when you "go offshore," and the same is true for people from the United Kingdom and Canada. But there are no—we repeat, no—outright and explicit prohibitions against American, British, or Canadian nationals engaging in a slew of offshore financial activity. It is legal and legitimate to invest offshore. We'll explain that in Chapter 4.

Offshore bank accounts, investments, and other financial activities offshore are *completely* legal under U.S. law. *The Wall Street Journal* reported in early 2006, "Many wealthy individuals are turning to foreign entities, such as offshore trusts and insurance policies, as part of their tax planning and asset protection strategies. Although U.S. citizens generally must report any foreign accounts and entities with the U.S. government each year, going offshore could add extra roadblocks on an audit trail."[1] You can expect U.S.-based lawyers, accountants, investment gurus, and insurance salespeople to do everything they can to discourage Americans from going where the best investments and the best asset protection reside—offshore. Why? Because they don't want to lose their clients.

There's one thing to keep in mind at all times: unlike almost all other nations, the United States taxes its citizens and permanent residents (green card holders) on their worldwide income regardless of their place of residence. This means that you could be a U.S. citizen who has lived in Ireland since you were a child, but you still owe taxes to the U.S. government. Crazy, isn't it? Many nations, like the United Kingdom and Canada, exempt their citizens from most or all taxes if they choose to live elsewhere.

This book tells you how to obey U.S. tax laws and file all the required reports, but ensure that a substantial portion of your assets and investments are located in the place where the best profits are—offshore.

A FINAL WORD ON THE OFFSHORE WORLD
Once more, offshore is simply a region beyond your native borders. When we refer to offshore, we're talking about offshore financial centers (often called offshore havens) that attract foreigners with their impressive financial opportunities.

---

[1] 11/23/05, Wall Street Journal, "IRS to Increase Audits Next Year," Tom Herman & Rachel Emma Silverman.

As you go through this book, you'll learn more about how you can use these offshore financial centers to *legally*

- Invest in the best-performing markets worldwide.

- Put an iron fortress around your wealth.

- Cut back on your tax bills.

- Secure real financial privacy.

- Diversify your wealth in many currencies.

- Safeguard your assets from crises.

The following chapters will show you how.

CHAPTER

2

AN OFFSHORE BANK ACCOUNT: YOUR GATE-WAY TO WORLD PROFITS

If you think of your offshore education as a swimming lesson, establishing an offshore bank account is the equivalent of learning how to float. It's safe, it's easy, and it's an important first step in establishing your financial self offshore. You can use this account for investment purposes or for simple asset protection—plus, it's a great way to stash a bit of cash abroad, just in case. Having such an account offers multiple benefits. The top three are investment and currency diversification, financial privacy, and some asset protection. This is the offshore trifecta!

A WORLD OF PROFITS AWAITS

Your offshore bank account will allow you to explore, with few restrictions, the far reaches of the vast and diverse financial universe safely and privately. Imagine a journey going from the bond markets of Korea to the stock exchanges of Eastern Europe, from ultra-private Liechtenstein trust arrangements to the most successful funds, from unique commodity investments to Caribbean corporations, from Israeli nanotech start-ups to age-old European blue chips, from the mysterious and secretive world of offshore mutual funds to tax-free Swiss gold accounts, from Isle of Man insurance contracts to Danish multicurrency investment accounts, from uniquely structured tax-free Austrian funds to Bulgarian mortgages—it's a vast and wide-open universe with limitless profits awaiting you.

With one phone call or a click of your mouse, an offshore bank account will allow you to:

1. Privately trade stocks, bonds, CDs, precious metals, and currencies in markets everywhere. We're talking about CDs that have historically paid up to 15 percent after currency gains and funds traded on exchanges that soared into double- and triple-digit returns in the past few years.

2. Diversify your assets among multiple currencies that will appreciate in value during the volatile times ahead.

U.S. Citizens Take Note

We do not recommend purchasing mutual funds in an offshore account because of the onerous tax consequences. Instead, you should consider purchasing them using a variable annuity or an offshore IRA. We'll discuss these options and the additional tax implications in Chapters 4 and 5.

It's Nobody's Business but Yours

In addition to the investment opportunities we just mentioned, an offshore bank account offers yet another benefit: a majority of offshore banks guarantee greater privacy than is available in the United States these days.

In the last 20 years, we've witnessed serious attacks on personal wealth in the U.S. The U.S. government has all but abolished domestic financial privacy. In fact, it's even gone a step further and reversed the burden of proof. If you are accused of wrongdoing, it is up to you to prove your innocence.

What ever happened to the idea of being presumed innocent until proven guilty? Say good-bye to the good old days. Let's face it: privacy is dead in America.

However, you can take steps to reestablish your financial privacy. And one step is to set up a bank account offshore. To maximize your privacy, there are two simple things you should consider when selecting an offshore bank:

- Avoid using an offshore bank that has branches located in your home country, especially if you live in the United States. This is to ensure optimal privacy. U.S. courts have been known to threaten to shut down U.S. bank branches or confiscate their funds if their offshore parent bank fails to comply with a U.S. court order.

- Use your offshore account only for offshore financial activity. Do not use your offshore checkbook to pay the water bill or the cable bill. That keeps personal offshore bank checks bearing your name from going through the

U.S. or Canadian banking system. Restrict yourself to personal cash withdrawals from your offshore account. Bank fees for international check clearing are costly and create recorded links that undermine privacy.

If personal privacy does not concern you, you can contact a foreign bank that has branches in the U.S. such as Royal Bank of Scotland or HSBC. Or you can choose a major U.S. bank like Citibank with offshore branches. In either case, this allows you to go offshore without leaving home. Be aware, however, that this option offers you little asset protection or privacy, given the bank's presence in the U.S. It's cut-and-dried: if it's in the United States, then it falls under U.S. legal jurisdiction. No two ways about it.

The Truth about "Bank Secrecy"

Bank secrecy has not been "eliminated," as the news media might imply. A realistic way to view bank secrecy today is to think of it as a strong safeguard against prying official or private eyes peering into your financial affairs. Of course this won't work if you're suspected of being involved in a serious crime, especially drug trafficking, terrorism, tax evasion, or money laundering.

Bank secrecy should not be used to hide from the U.S. government. It actually serves legitimate purposes, such as shielding honest individuals from corrupt business partners, tenants or family members. Also, it provides access to investments that may be unavailable or restricted in their own countries, and it can provide strong asset protection that is not available in their home country.

Indeed, bank secrecy laws do exist in many reputable offshore havens. Panama, Nevis, Belize, Liechtenstein, Austria, and Gibraltar—to name a few—have official bank privacy laws, which are waived only in criminal cases and usually only under court order. Unlike the United States, where average bank employees can (and in certain circumstances must) reveal your personal financial details, many offshore nations impose fines and prison sentences on bank employees who violate the privacy of account holders. That's the outstanding feature of an offshore account.

WRAP YOUR ACCOUNT WITH A SAFETY BLANKET

In addition to the investment opportunities we mentioned previously, an offshore account offers some asset protection. People do not have to know that you have assets offshore, and we strongly recommend that you do not reveal this information to anyone. The fact is, you don't need secrecy to protect your wealth against lawsuits. Should you end up in court, you may have to disclose an offshore account as part of a statement of your total assets and liabilities. However, once your opponents realize that your money is thousands of miles away, they are fully aware of how difficult it might be for them to gain access to it. This factor alone can facilitate out-of-court settlements and put an end to lengthy lawsuits. Either way, you win.

On top of all these benefits, some offshore banks even offer Visa, MasterCard, or other global credit cards that can be linked or traced to your account. They are more expensive than U.S. cards. Your offshore bank can deduct your monthly credit card charges from your account balance. This allows you to pay bills offshore, make deposits, and pay with your offshore account outside your home country.

Factors to Consider for Your Offshore Account

The first step in opening your offshore bank account is to decide where the best place for your account might be. While selecting an offshore bank may sound exotic or even difficult, the truth is that it's no different from picking a local banker. You should check out the bank's reputation, financial condition, fees, services, and related costs. Also, ensure that the bank welcomes foreigners and is experienced with foreigners' needs. Its staff members must speak fluent English. The last thing you want is to open your account, only to find out later that none of the account managers understood your instructions.

It is also important that you understand the fee structure of these banks. Offshore bank fees can be expensive, more than what Americans usually pay at home. Crunch the numbers and find out what your net profit (or loss) might be.

TOP 10 QUESTIONS TO ASK AN OFFSHORE BANK

Once you decide on an offshore bank, ask and get answers to these questions before you finally agree to do business with that bank:

1. What types of accounts are available to international investors?

2. Are there any restrictions on foreigners' investments?

3. What taxes will be withheld from my investment income?

4. What investments are considered part of the bank's balance sheet and available to the bank's creditors (including depositors) in the event of the bank's insolvency?

5. What are the fees for securities transactions and custody?

6. What other fees may apply to the account?

7. Is my account insured by law or otherwise against loss in the event of the bank's insolvency?

8. How do I transact business with the bank—are telephone, fax, or e-mail orders accepted?

9. Is Internet online banking available and secure? If so, is this service available in English?

10. Will the bank send U.S. customers a year-end statement showing any taxable interest paid?

Also, invest the time up front to check the bank's financial standing and do due diligence. If you aren't sure where to start, visit www.fitchratings.com and www.moodys.com.

Where in the World Should You Bank?

Keep in mind that there are a vast number of offshore regions that could suit your particular banking needs. But just to give you some ideas, we've included a list of offshore regions recommended for offshore banking.

1. *Switzerland*—as long as minimums starting around $250,000 aren't a problem for you

2. *Liechtenstein*—again, as long as you can handle higher minimums

3. *Austria*—if you like the idea of banking confidentiality being written into the constitution

4. *Denmark*—if you're interested in innovative financial products and solid performance

5. *Singapore*—if you're interested in strong privacy laws and getting far beyond the EU Tax Savings Directive (if you're European)

6. *Hong Kong*—especially if you want to take advantage of Chinese and other investments

7. *Jersey*—if you specifically want to bank in the Channel Islands

8. *The Cayman Islands*—if financial privacy isn't a primary concern

Take the Time to Meet Your Banker— Develop a Lasting Relationship

It's always a good idea to visit the bank personally or at least meet with one of its account managers. In fact, nowadays, nearly every private offshore bank requires personal meetings. As in most business relationships, an initial personal contact is best. Moreover, it is important to understand most nations have anti-money-laundering laws similar to those in the United States or United Kingdom, which require new customers to appear personally when opening accounts.

These "know-your-customer" (KYC) rules are now standard policy and practice in international banking. Bank officials are keen on developing business, but they do not wish to deal with drug merchants, terrorists, criminals, or crooked politicians—and for good reason.

In addition to a face-to-face meeting, nearly all reputable offshore banks will require a new account applicant to produce positive identification, such as a passport and/or birth certificate; business and personal references; and a home country utility bill in his name. This is an indispensable requirement, as banks need proof of your current residence.

Important point: personal contact should be reciprocal. As soon as you open your account, get to know your assigned staff contact at the bank. Your banking contact should speak your language, understand your business, and be reliable. Request the name of a backup contact at the bank who knows who you are in case your usual representative is not available.

Here's your offshore bank checklist:

1. Be ready for a personal meeting; bring all the necessary supporting documentation.

2. Get your assigned bank staff member's contact information.

3. Get the bank staff member's backup contact to use during his absence.

4. Get the bank's emergency telephone numbers, fax, e-mail addresses, and civic address.

5. Obtain a written statement of the bank's policies.

Some offshore banks demand that depositors sign a letter allowing the bank to release account details to foreign investigators, thus waiving the depositor's rights under bank secrecy laws. If an offshore bank you are considering makes such a request, take your business elsewhere.

What Are Numbered Accounts?

Let's be clear about one thing: there is no such thing as a totally secret or "numbered account" anywhere in the world. Even in the nations with the strongest bank privacy laws, such as Austria or Switzerland, a bank account holder's real name is on record somewhere. Even if a bank account is in a corporate name or in the name of a trust, there is always a piece of paper (or computer file) that can be traced to the real owner, especially if government agents are investigating alleged criminal activities.

You will, however, be pleased to know that once you open an account, and satisfy all of the "Know Your Customer" requirements, some banks will allow you to correspond with them using only a set of numbers. This adds the element of privacy to all communications—as only the bank will have all details relating to you.

CHOOSE THE RIGHT BANK FOR YOUR NEEDS

Like domestic U.S. banks, international banks specialize in the following areas:

1. Taking money deposits and lending to businesses (commercial banks)

2. Taking money deposits and lending to private individuals (savings and loans)

3. Buying and holding investments for private individuals (private banks)

Know what type of account you need. If you want only a small international nest egg and you don't plan to actively trade and invest using your account, your best option is an international building society, a savings and loan, or a commercial bank. Interest rates are usually higher and fees much lower. Unfortunately, most of these banks, such as Abbey National in the United Kingdom, will not accept accounts directly from Americans unless they live in the United Kingdom, offering their savings and mortgage business only to British residents. Other jurisdictions will allow nonresidents to open accounts.

If you want to do business internationally, you will need an international commercial bank that specializes in business financing, multiple currency dealings, and merchant payment solutions. If you are an active investor or you wish to open a larger account, chances are that you would be better served by a private bank.

Offshore Account Minimums

The opening account minimums vary from bank to bank. If you are looking for a private bank, the lowest minimum we are aware of is around $50,000. For a private account in Switzerland or Liechtenstein, an opening minimum is between $100,000 and $250,000. And for larger Swiss banks such as Julius Baer, you need about $1 million to open an account.

Private Customized Bank Service Just for You

Offshore banking services are often handled by the private banking departments of offshore commercial banks or by private banks that cater solely to a private banking clientele.

Countries like Switzerland have been doing this type of specialized banking for centuries, and many other havens have been doing it for decades. Only recently have U.S. banks caught up with this trend, trolling for wealthy clients who demand personalized treatment.

The private banking department of a commercial bank functions as an exclusive "bank within a bank," with separate books and records and special operating procedures. Each private bank account holder can rely on account managers or marketing officers who have access to specialists around the world who are able to provide personal money management, financial advice, and investment services to their high-net-worth clients.

Very good private bankers are unique in that they have knowledge and understanding of their clients' personal and business backgrounds, their sources of wealth, and how they want to use their private bank accounts. They also understand international clients and know how to meet their growing needs. They often work U.S. hours, speak fluent English, and aim to help you accomplish your personalized goals, be they wealth accumulation or protection.

Opening and Funding Your Account

As we mentioned earlier in this chapter, under internationally accepted know-your-customer policies, banks worldwide now require customers to fully identify themselves. Before they open a new account for you, the bank must know who you are and will request documented proof concerning the source of the funds you plan to deposit.

To illustrate, let's say you sold your vacation home in Turkey for €210,000 and you plan to deposit those funds in a private bank in Denmark. The bank will require proof that the money to be deposited comes from the sale of a property. If you are unable to furnish this proof, it will most likely refuse to open the account. Understand that the bank isn't being difficult, nor is it refusing your business. It's more a question of vigilance on its part about accepting suspicious funds.

When applying for your account at a private bank, have the following information ready:

- A *detailed application.* This will show your name and address, the type of account you wish to open, the currency in which you want your funds to be denominated, and a request for a debit/credit card. To satisfy know-your-customer rules, you must prove your identity and nationality (usually with a passport or certified birth certificate), and provide a utility bill to confirm your residential address.

- *Investor profile.* This is a statement of your investment objectives, investment experience, and the investment risk approach that you prefer.

- *Source of funds.* You will need to specify the source of your funds and, in some cases, obtain a reference letter from a bank in your home country stipulating that the funds are legitimate.

- *The identity of your beneficiary.* It is possible that in the event of your death, your account and other related investments will not be released to your loved ones without costly legal proceedings. To avoid this, you must designate your spouse, your partner, or some other person as an account beneficiary. This designation is revocable, so you can always add a new beneficiary or change beneficiaries. For banks that don't offer this option, the alternative is to make your intended beneficiary a co-owner of the account, which gives survivorship rights in the event of your death.

OFFSHORE BANK ACCOUNTS—YOUR OPTIONS

Offshore banks offer a greater variety of account types than most home-country domestic banks. The terms describing a particular type of account may vary from one bank to another. However the two most common private bank accounts are a managed account and an investment account.

An investment account at a private bank typically starts with an opening minimum account of $50,000 to $100,000. This type of account allows you to invest in the bank's chosen investments, such as stocks, bonds, commodities, currencies, etc., with the bank's assistance and management. Your account is directed by an account manager at the bank. You are able to set your investment risk level—conservative, moderate, or aggressive. Your manager will find an investment mix that meets your objectives and financial goals.

A managed account is similar to the investment account, but, with this type of account, you choose your investments. Buy and sell instructions are phoned or faxed to your bank representative. You may also hold commodities in the name of the bank for the sake of privacy, if this is important to you. Managed accounts can be opened at a variety of private banks with an opening minimum of $100,000 to $250,000.

A Word about Fees

Before you sign the management agreement or fund an account at any bank, it's important that you understand how the bank will charge for management performance, as well as what normal transaction fees are. You also need to know about additional offshore bank fees that might come into play.

While every bank has a slightly different fee structure, here is a rough guide as to the typical fees. Most banks will charge 1 percent to 1.75 percent annually to manage your account. This is applicable to the investment account explained earlier. In addition to the annual management fee, the banks also charge a custodian/safekeeping fee of approximately 0.25 to 0.40 percent annually to cover administrative functions such as sending statements, handling reporting, etc. There may also be transaction fees when you buy and sell investments in your account. On average, expect to spend 1.75 to 2.6 percent per year on account fees.

Bank fees are negotiable if you have a sizable account of $1 million or more.

Warning: Reporting Your Offshore Bank Account

Under no circumstances should you hide reportable income in your offshore account! Nor should you use an offshore bank credit card as an unreported piggy bank to conceal income or personal expenses. It's illegal—that's the plain and simple truth. The IRS has targeted the abuse of offshore credit cards and their holders, and many of them have been prosecuted.

If you are a U.S. citizen, you must inform the IRS about any offshore account over which you have direct or indirect control. This includes any international business bank accounts for which you are an authorized signatory. Under penalty of perjury, you must reveal your account on your annual U.S. income tax return (IRS Form 1040), and you must complete form TD F90-22.1 by June 30 of each year. The TD F90-22.1 should be mailed to the U.S. Department of Treasury, PO Box 32621, Detroit, MI 48232-0621.

Offshore banking solutions are not about avoiding your legal reporting obligations or evading taxes in any way. Don't even consider it.

YOUR MONEY NEEDS A PASSPORT, TOO—HOW TO TRANSFER MONEY OFFSHORE

In the United States, there is virtually no way in which funds amounting to $10,000 or more can be transferred without some federal cash reporting law coming into play. By law, funds in that amount or higher are automatically reported to the U.S. Treasury by electronic means by the bank on which they are drawn. This should not concern you, because, as we mentioned earlier, you should never move money offshore for the purposes of avoiding legal reporting requirements or tax obligations. This is the wrong reason for moving your funds to an offshore location, and you run the risk of being prosecuted.

Still, a major concern for first-time offshore bank account clients and investors is, "How do I safely and legally transfer my cash and assets to my new bank?" Let's look at the options:

- *Wires.* Wires are the easiest way to move funds from your home-country bank to your offshore bank. However, not all U.S. banks are good at handling international wire transfers, and it may take several days for the transfer to be completed.

- *Checks.* You can write a domestic check to move funds offshore. But, remember that it can take many days, if not weeks, for a foreign check to clear the international banking system.

Wiring Money to Your Account

When wiring money to your new offshore account, you should wire the money in your home currency. When the funds arrive at the bank, you can opt to transfer them to a different currency of your choice. For example, if your home currency is the U.S. dollar, but you wish to fund your offshore account in Swiss francs, you should wire your deposit in U.S. dollars and then authorize the offshore bank to convert those U.S. dollars to Swiss francs. In many cases, this can save you foreign exchange transaction fees.

If you physically move $10,000 or more in cash, you must file the appropriate forms with the IRS or the U.S. Customs and Border Protection Agency. In almost all instances, the bank or transferring agency will automatically file the forms for you. Failure to report this is a very serious matter, as the cash can be confiscated on the spot at the airport. Be aware, too, that this reporting requirement also applies to the transport of cash equivalents, including traveler's checks, bearer bonds, and other negotiable securities. In addition to the necessary U.S. reporting requirement regarding cash, most offshore banks will not accept cash deposits, the reason being that they need to know the source of the funds. Because cash is not easy to document, they just say no. The days of investors arriving on a small Caribbean airstrip with a suitcase or two of cash are history.

You should also be aware that it is a crime to break up cash transfers into smaller amounts with the intent of avoiding the $10,000 reporting requirement. This is called structuring. A series of smaller transfers under $10,000 will attract the bank's attention. In fact, most U.S. banks now have automatic software programs that constantly review bank account use patterns.

OUTSIDE OF NORMAL BANKING: SAFEKEEPING ARRANGEMENTS

There's one last solution that we'd like to mention in this chapter. It's not a direct bank account, but the service is quite useful, and it's often tied to offshore banks. We are talking about private safe-deposit boxes or private vault services. These boxes can often prove useful. For example, valuables purchased outside the United States, like valuable documents, that are placed directly into an offshore safe-deposit box or private security vault are not legally reportable. At first glance, you may think it would be difficult to keep valuables or documents so far from home. To avoid having to visit the box personally each time you wish to add or remove valuables, you could give a local attorney or other trusted intermediary a limited power of attorney, which would legally allow them to do this for you.

Note, too, that several foreign banks offer custodial arrangements for clients. This means that they will maintain custody of cash, securities, or precious metals on your behalf. With regard to legal U.S. reporting requirements, custodial arrangements fall into a gray area. Some experts argue that such an arrangement may be nonreportable because the bank is merely safekeeping the assets. However, such an arrangement usually exists in tandem with an actual bank account, and assets may be moved between the accounts at your instructions. In this case, the custodial arrangement resembles a reportable account relationship more than it does merely renting and using a safe-deposit box or private vault.

You can also choose a private vault instead of a bank. Private vault companies are nonfinancial institutions and, as such, are subject to fewer record-keeping and disclosure requirements. A few even permit anonymous vault rentals, and almost all of these companies honor power of attorney arrangements.

One last point to keep in mind is that materials held in a safe-deposit box or private vault are not ordinarily insured against theft or other loss. You can purchase supplemental insurance, but the existence and location of the assets must be disclosed to the insurer. Food for thought.

Safe-deposit boxes and private vaults aren't for everyone. Only you can decide if this solution fills the bill for you.

A Final Word on Offshore Bank Accounts

Opening an offshore account truly is the first and most important step you can make offshore. So don't cut corners. Take your time and decide which offshore location, type of bank account, and account manager best suits your particular needs. And while you're searching for your ideal offshore bank, make sure to:

1. Visit your offshore location of choice before you commit to it.
2. Check out the bank's reputation.
3. Come prepared and ask questions.
4. Bring the appropriate documentation.
5. Make sure you can afford your chosen bank's fees.
6. Find out if your chosen bank offers the type of bank account you're seeking.
7. Get to know the person or team who will be managing your account.

And remember that you absolutely must report your offshore banking activities to the IRS! So before you set up your offshore bank account, make sure you're prepared to fill out the appropriate forms.

Now, building upon this foundation, let's take a look at useful legal entities for you and your money.

CHAPTER

3

USEFUL LEGAL ENTITIES
FOR YOU AND
YOUR MONEY

Offshore legal entities can provide a fortress for your wealth. Most people don't really understand how these structures work. Don't be discouraged with this particular chapter. It may sound complicated at first, but it really isn't.

In this chapter, we'll explain a variety of legal terms and structures. You may already be familiar with some of them, whereas others will be totally new. Remember, these are easy concepts to learn. After all, you aren't studying for a law degree—you're just learning your way around the offshore world. Here you will learn how trusts, family foundations, international business corporations, and limited liability companies work. Before you dive into this chapter, you may want to review your personal goals so that you can make the most of it.

Trusts: Solid Asset Protection Made Easy

Trusts are unique. They've been around since the reign of Caesar Augustus and they continue to flourish. Trusts offer solid asset protection, providing the means for financing your future and that of your family.

Trusts operate on the basic premise that the best way to protect your wealth, whether it be cash, property, assets, or something else, is to give it away—give it away to a trust, that is.

How Does a Trust Work?

In simple terms, a trust is a three-way legal device. With this device, a person or a couple takes certain possessions—including real estate, cars, boats, investments, cash, collectibles, and other assets—and legally transfers the ownership of those possessions to the trust. The person who funds the trust is referred to as the grantor; he is granting his assets to the legal structure.

The trust is directed by another person, who is referred to as the trustee. The trustee is responsible for making sure that the grantor's wishes are carried out and that the trust is properly managed.

The trustee manages the trust (and the assets it holds title to) for the benefit of one or more people. These people are known as the beneficiaries of the trust. The person who funds the trust (the grantor) determines who the beneficiaries will be. In a nutshell, the grantor gives the assets to the trustee to administer for the benefit of named beneficiaries.

This is a very simple explanation. The possible variations on this basic idea are almost endless. You can have any number of grantors, trustees, and beneficiaries. You can place any type of asset into the trust. Most people create a trust to serve a specific purpose; in many cases, people use them for estate planning.

It is possible for the grantor of a trust to also be a beneficiary of the trust. However, you should consult with an attorney who has expertise in this area before you move forward with such an arrangement. By giving up your assets to the trust but then listing yourself as a beneficiary of those assets, you could be reducing the asset protection provided by the trust structure.

The Best of Both Worlds

The creation of a trust is also rather simple. It starts with a written statement called a declaration, which, as we explained earlier, directs one person (the trustee) to take possession of, and hold title to, the property, which is to be used for the benefit of other people (the beneficiaries). Once the document is signed and the property is transferred to the trustee, the grantor no longer owns or manages that property. However, the grantor will save very little, if anything, on U.S. taxes by transferring his assets to the trust during his lifetime. It is important to work with a U.S. tax attorney when creating the trust to ensure compliance with all U.S. regulations and reporting requirements.

There are two types of trust that you can create: revocable and irrevocable. If the trust is revocable, this means that the grantor can cancel the relationship at some point in the future and take possession of the assets. In addition, the beneficiaries of the trust can be changed. This is a slightly more flexible structure, but one that still provides asset protection.

If you create an irrevocable trust, this means that the assets are permanently given to the beneficiaries. Once the beneficiaries are named, they typically cannot be changed. This structure, because of its permanence, has the highest degree of asset protection, yet it is also the most rigid.

That's why a trust is an ideal tool for asset protection. Once your assets have been given to the trustee, they belong to the trust, not to you. And because you no longer legally own the trust assets, your creditors can't seize them. We'll explain more about this in a moment.

How a Trust Works

Consider this scenario: You decide to create a trust to provide for your children, or to provide for yourself once you retire. You become the grantor. The uses for which a trust can be formed are as broad as you can imagine, but a trust can't be used for illegal purposes. There are many different kinds of trusts, depending on the objectives of the trust: owning a business or a home, taking care of someone after you're gone, or just protecting your investments so they can't be attacked.

You create a written trust declaration that tells the trustee what you, as the grantor, wish to have happen and who will receive the benefits. The trustee then manages the trust assets by investing them wisely, hopefully producing profits, so that the beneficiaries can be paid income. The beneficiaries of the trust will receive distributions from the trust assets, and they will have what is called an "equitable title" to those benefits. Note, however, that beneficiaries of your trust do not own, nor have the right to control, any of those assets.

The Smith Family

John and Mary have been married for nearly 42 years and have four children. They've done well for themselves. They own a few properties and a boat, and they collect classic cars—historic Buicks, to be exact. They have a sizable retirement nest egg, and, at the moment, things are great. But John is worried about what Mary will do when he is gone—how she'll deal with all of their assets. He calls Bob, his lawyer, and tells him to set up a trust to take care of Mary and the kids if anything happens to him. Bob is an unusual lawyer and John trusts him, so he elects Bob to be the trustee. The papers are signed. John turns over title to most of his assets, including $450,000 in shares of XYZ stock. The trust is funded, and John has conveyed his wishes to Bob: in the event of his death, he wants to be sure that his wife, his children, and their lifelong friend Jane will be financially independent. Eight months later, John suddenly passes away. Since John had previously set up the trust, there is no fuss. The trust outlives John and does not have to be settled through messy probate court. Bob follows John's instructions and begins to pay out distributions to the beneficiaries.

AN OFFSHORE ASSET PROTECTION TRUST— PROTECTION YOU WON'T FIND DOMESTICALLY

You now understand the basic trust structure. You also know that one of the main benefits of a trust is that it gives you rock-solid asset protection because, as we explained earlier, once you place your assets in an irrevocable trust, they don't belong to you anymore. Personal claims against you can no longer be made against that trust property.

Before we go further, let us give you an example of a possible scenario—we'll use the Smith Family again. Let's suppose that after John created the trust for Mary, their kids, and Jane, another party, Max, sued John for $450,000. This lawsuit occurred before John's death. Max claims that John failed to carry out the terms of a business deal and that John had pledged the XYZ stock as collateral for the deal. John answers that he made no such deal, and, in any case, he had set up the trust and transferred the XYZ shares well before he and Max had any business dealings. John's assertion proves to be correct, and the suit is dropped because the shares were not John's to pledge at the time Max alleges the deal occurred.

As you can see, a trust can be very useful for shielding your assets. You can further improve the strength of that shield by going offshore. Yes, you can set up a trust in your home country, but an offshore asset protection trust (OAPT) gives you far greater asset protection when that trust is based in an offshore asset haven.

That extra level of protection results from the fact that the trust and most of its assets are located outside your home country, in an asset haven of your choice. This means that even if a creditor or claimant obtains a judgment in a U.S. court, that court may have no power or jurisdiction over the offshore trust or its assets.

If the judgment holder really wants to go to the time and expense, he or they must file suit against the offshore trust in the foreign country, paying for lawyers there, and he or they must be able to show that the trust is invalid under the foreign country's law. The sheer cost and complexity of this will cause most U.S. plaintiff's lawyers to either decline the case or recommend settlement for pennies on the dollar.

An offshore asset protection trust is a special, targeted form of trust that is created by a grantor who lives in one nation but creates and places the trust under the laws of another nation. Because the trust is governed by the laws of the nation in which it is registered or administered, this constitutes an extra layer of protection for the trust grantor's business and personal assets within the trust. And an offshore APT discourages would-be creditors, lawsuits, and other financial liabilities.

Here are a few key benefits of an offshore APT:

- *Greater protection.* Under the laws of haven nations, assets placed in an OAPT have far more protection than they would have under U.S. trust law. The law in such countries provides an asset protection "safe harbor" that is unavailable in the United States and other nations. With an OAPT, the trust assets are held outside the jurisdiction of your local or home-country courts.

- *The need to start over.* An OAPT is in another country. Foreign courts often will not recognize U.S. or other nations' domestic court orders. A creditor who is trying to collect must relitigate the original claim in a local court with local lawyers. He may have to post a bond and pay legal expenses for all parties if he loses. The overwhelming legal complexity and costs of such an international collection effort are likely to stop all but the most determined adversaries.

- *Minimal needs.* An offshore APT doesn't have to be complex. It can require little more than the signing of documents and opening a trust bank account managed by your local trustee in your offshore bank. Offshore and trust banks can provide experienced trust officers and staff to handle trust matters and make investments. International banks have U.S. dollar-denominated accounts, often with better interest rates than U.S. banks offer.

- *Fast acting.* The statute of limitations imposed on a foreign creditor's lawsuit varies, but in many offshore centers it begins to run from the date your OAPT was established. Some haven nations, such as the Cook Islands, have a limit of one year for starting claims. Others impose a limit of within two years for filing claims by certain creditors. It may take a creditor longer than that just to discover the existence of an offshore APT.

- *Better investments.* An offshore APT is a great platform for diversifying your investments. It gives you access to the world's best investment opportunities without your home nation's restrictions, such as those that the SEC imposes on U.S. persons. An offshore APT can also buy attractive life insurance and annuity products that are not available in the United States.

- *Confidentiality.* The OAPT provides greater privacy and confidentiality, and it avoids the probate process. It also gives you flexibility in conducting your affairs in case of illness or personal disability, allows easy transfer of asset titles, and avoids currency controls. An OAPT is also a good substitute for, or supplement to, costly professional liability insurance or even a prenuptial agreement, giving strong protection for your heirs' inheritance.

- *Estate planning.* An offshore APT can achieve the same estate planning goals as domestic strategies, including the use of bypass trust provisions to minimize estate taxes for a husband and wife, allowing maximum use of gift tax exemptions through planned giving, and providing for maintenance and tax-free income for a surviving spouse.

Where in the World Should You Set Up a Trust?

As with offshore bank accounts, there are many offshore trust-friendly locations. Here are a few of our favorites. But please, keep in mind that not all trust-friendly locations are created equal. See Chapter 8 for more information on any one of these locations.

- Panama

- Liechtenstein

- Singapore

- Nevis

- Jersey

- Cook Islands

- Anguilla

Transferring Assets to Your Offshore Asset Protection Trust

An offshore APT gives better protection than a domestic trust because whenever your assets are physically located within your home country, they are within the reach of local courts. That means that domestic trusts may not always be protected from domestic judgments. It's important to note that placing title to property that remains in your home country in the name of a foreign trust and trustee offers very little protection.

Do Not Put U.S. Property in an Offshore Trust

You can legally transfer the title to a U.S. residence to an offshore asset protection trust; however, should a judgment go against you, the court could order that your home be seized to satisfy the judgment. The title may be foreign, but the property is local. Keep this in mind when deciding how to put your offshore APT to best use. In this case, a domestic LLC or trust would offer the same degree of protection.

If tangible assets such as cash, funds, stocks, or collectibles are actually transferred to a foreign haven—using an offshore trust account or a trustee's safe-deposit box—a home-country creditor will have a hard time gaining access to them, even if he discovers that you have an offshore trust. That's the wonderful thing about the extra layer of protection. If you are moving cash, investments, or other such assets into a trust, your trustee will need to open a bank account in the name of the trust to hold those assets.

For protection, the OAPT and its trustee should employ an offshore bank that is not a branch or affiliate of a bank within your home country. This helps insulate your offshore bank officials and your OAPT account from pressure from home-country lawyers or information snoops, government or otherwise.

Even with this better financial privacy, there may sometimes be a tactical advantage to letting a harassing party know that your assets are offshore and way beyond his reach. The cost and difficulty of pursuit may well discourage him or lead to a settlement.

Offshore Asset Protection—for Almost Anyone

At various points in this book, we've discussed shielding your assets from unwarranted attacks. Offshore asset protection, while not 100 percent foolproof, offers you the opportunity to build real safeguards around your wealth, when you follow the proper steps and work with reputable professionals. Wealth protection is a necessity if you're in a high-risk business or in the medical profession. Even just having money could make you the target of a frivolous lawsuit. We all know that more lawsuits are filed each year in the United States than in any other country. You certainly need to take precautions.

Remember: You *can't* use offshore structures to evade taxes, fail to comply with reporting requirements, or conduct any type of illegal activity. If you engage in illegal activity, all asset havens will act to expose that activity immediately—including freezing funds, turning information over to government officials, and so on. We repeat: don't try anything illegal offshore. It won't work.

The Price Tag for an Offshore APT

We'd love to be able to quote you a price. But the cost of creating an asset protection trust in an offshore haven varies. The cost is usually based on the complexity of the structure. However, almost all offshore trusts have an up-front creation fee and an annual maintenance fee that covers the trustee's time and effort to keep the trust running efficiently year after year.

A few years ago, *BusinessWeek* estimated that "as a rule of thumb you should have a net worth of around $500,000" or more in order to justify a foreign APT. The magazine cited expert fees for establishing and administering such trusts as running as high as $50,000, with some trustees demanding a percentage of the total value of the assets to be transferred. While trusts nowadays cost a lot less than that, the $500,000 asset threshold is still a good benchmark.

While high costs may once have been the rule, the costs for simple and less complex OAPTs are now substantially lower. Offshore trusts are no longer the monopoly of the very rich. Most reputable trust companies will look at your particular estate, create a plan, then quote a price that will fit your needs. Be wary of a trust provider who offers one solution to everyone. We call these "cookie-cutter" trusts, and many times those solutions may not best suit your needs.

Should You Have a Trust?

Because trusts have been around for so long, there are lots of laws and rules that apply to them. In addition, tax collectors have another whole set of tax rules about trusts: how they must be formed and reported, and how much taxes should be paid if any are due. While a simple trust may not cost much to set up, a more complicated trust can be costly.

Among other things, a trust can

- Conduct a commercial or professional business.

- Own and invest in real estate, currencies, stocks, bonds, negotiable instruments, and personal property.

- Provide for a spouse, minor children, or the elderly.

- Pay medical, educational, and other expenses.

- Make financial support available in an emergency, for retirement, or during marriage or divorce, or even carry out prenuptial agreements.

- Protect your home and family while lowering your inheritance taxes and avoiding the muddle of the probate court process.

The only way to know if you should create a trust is to consult professionals who know how to analyze your financial and family situation. They can tell you what's best for your particular case. Again, beware of some fraudulent trust promoters who make grandiose claims about what a trust can do.

The Family Foundation

There is a unique asset protection and wealth distribution legal entity called a *family foundation*. A family foundation allows you to manage your estate for the benefit of children, parents, grandparents, or other relatives. The person or persons who set up the foundation also manage it and its assets for other family members and themselves.

Before we continue, we want to state outright that this type of foundation is not the same as the things that Americans know as vehicles for donating cash and assets to charity in return for big tax breaks and deductions against U.S. income taxes. Those are foundations such as the Ford, Rockefeller, or Gates Foundations. The type of family foundations we are discussing here are *not* nonprofit, tax-exempt organizations.

The family foundation we discuss here is an independent fund consisting of assets donated by the founder, usually the oldest member of the family, for the specific, noncommercial purpose of family support and assistance to relatives and heirs.

Difference between a Trust and a Family Foundation

With a trust, the owner of the assets gives them away to a trustee to manage. In this case, the trustee acquires legal ownership of the assets but is bound by law to manage them in the best interests of the beneficiaries.

With a foundation, the owner of the assets sets aside the assets for a particular purpose, which is usually to provide for family members. Those assets are managed by a designated board of directors and governed by a set of bylaws created by the founder. This is a different relationship from having a trustee manage your trust based on a letter outlining your wishes.

Another small yet important distinction is that foundation beneficiaries must be relatives through either blood or marriage. With trusts, the grantor can make anyone a beneficiary—a friend, business associate, girlfriend, or anyone else. Note that the family foundation's purpose can be even broader, including religious and charitable goals. The most common use is for a so-called pure family foundation, dedicated to the financial management and personal welfare of one or more named and related families and their members as the beneficiaries.

Unlike other legal entities we talk about here, the family foundation has no shareholders, partners, owners, or members—it has only beneficiaries who are family members linked together by blood or by marriage. It can be set up to be either limited in time or perpetual. The foundation and its beneficiaries' interests can't be assigned, sold, or attached by family members' personal creditors. Only foundation assets are liable for foundation debts.

Whether it's engaged in commercial activities or in investing, the family foundation's activities must be directed toward earning income for the noncommercial purpose of supporting the family. The founder's name or the family name need not be made public. Foundations may be created by deed, under the terms of a will, or by a common agreement among family members. A fam-

The Gordons

David and Cheryl Gordon are parents and grandparents. David Gordon is an astute businessman and investor who has made millions of dollars. Cheryl is an award-winning author of children's books. Their combined activities have generated a few million dollars over the years. They decide to form a family foundation in Panama. The foundation is administered by a trust company in Panama, where its offshore investments are tax-free in Panama, with a U.S. tax accounting firm taking care of the reporting. When David and Cheryl pass on, the directors of the foundation will provide for their eldest daughter and their youngest son, and there is a mechanism for appointing new directors. Good investments keep the income rolling in, and this makes everyone happy. The foundation can go on forever—with the children receiving distributions from the foundation.

ily foundation can be more useful than a trust, since it can operate more freely. The board can make decisions about the assets without having to consult a trustee or anyone else, as long as it acts in accordance with the foundation's purposes as expressed in the bylaws.

Locations for Family Foundations and Reporting Considerations

The family foundation we've just outlined exists only offshore. The concept originated in Liechtenstein some years ago, and it has now been copied and adopted in the laws of Panama and most recently by the Bahamas and St. Kitts and Nevis.

Depending on the nature of the family foundation's activities, how the family foundation documents are drafted, and American tax laws, the IRS may treat it as a trust or as a company with similar IRS reporting requirements and tax implications. If you're interested in exploring the creation of a family foundation, you should get top-quality tax and legal advice, both in your home country and in the offshore nation where you decide to locate your family foundation. The family foundation is definitely worth considering for both strong asset protection and flexibility in administering wealth.

LIMITED LIABILITY COMPANY

This is another offshore legal entity that is well worth mentioning in this chapter—the Offshore Limited Liability Company (OLLC). A limited liability company brings together the features of a corporation and a partnership, although it's not the same as either one.

You can use an offshore LLC to:

- Hold an offshore investment portfolio managed by yourself, an offshore bank or independent asset manager

- Operate an offshore business

- Own offshore real estate

- Trade and Re-invoice

- Act as a holding company

In the LLC, the owners are called "members," not partners or shareholders. You may have one member or more, and the members can be individuals, corporations, or other LLCs.

Because the LLC is a separate entity like a corporation, owners have the liability protection of a corporation. This means that members cannot be held personally responsible for company debts unless they have signed a personal guarantee. In addition, LLCs offer a variety of ways to distribute company profits. And unlike international business corporations (discussed later in this chapter), the LLC requires no minutes or resolutions.

For greater asset protection, it's useful to have more than one member in the LLC. In addition, you should keep in mind that adding your spouse as an additional member does not offer dramatically more protection. However, having two unrelated members or additional family members, such as children, can increase the asset protection element.

Tax Benefits and More

For tax purposes, all business losses, profits, and expenses flow through the LLC to the individual members. That means that the individual LLC member must report his share of profits and losses annually as part of his income on Form 1040.

The good news is that double taxation (paying both corporate and individual taxes) is avoided—a real advantage. There is one limitation: an LLC is dissolved when a member dies or goes bankrupt.

Most offshore financial centers now allow the formation of LLCs. They are easy to create. To set up your own offshore LLC, you need

1. *Articles of organization.* These are filed with the government when you pay the required fees. Articles may be prepared by a local lawyer, or you can file them yourself.

2. *An operating agreement.* Much like corporate bylaws or partnership agreements, the operating agreement helps define your LLC's profit sharing, ownership, responsibilities, and ownership changes.

Another positive of an LLC is that overall, the required reporting is rather minimal. Depending on the jurisdiction you select, you may need to pay an annual registration fee for the LLC.

Using an LLC also enhances your personal privacy. For example, you can create a Nevis LLC and then open your offshore account in the name of the LLC. Should a snoop find your account, your name wouldn't appear on the documentation; instead, the name of your LLC would. Keep in mind that an LLC doesn't offer any U.S. tax savings, nor can you keep the LLC private from the U.S. government.

Where in the World Can You Set Up an LLC?

There are several offshore locations where you can set up an LLC, but the best jurisdictions we've found are

- Nevis

- Panama

- Anguilla

For example, one of the best jurisdictions for LLCs is Nevis, where there is a well-established LLC law. An LLC in Nevis can be set up in a matter of hours for about $1,000.

INTERNATIONAL BUSINESS CORPORATION

Many people have heard of an international business corporation, referred to as an IBC. Simply put, an IBC is a corporation that is registered in a foreign tax haven under local corporation laws. It's the same as a company anywhere with an "Inc." after its name, except that it's registered in another country. (Some nations do not use "Inc." to designate corporate status; each nation has its own version or equivalent of this abbreviation.)

An IBC can do business almost anywhere in the world, but it may not conduct business in the country in which it is registered.

For example, you wouldn't use a Belize IBC to do business in Belize. Usually you pay an initial incorporation fee and an annual maintenance fee to the country in which the company is being established—but no other local taxes apply.

Just as with U.S. corporations, with an offshore IBC, the same person can be a shareholder, director, president, agent, or any other company officer. It's not unusual for the true owner(s) to appoint local resident officers and directors. The beneficial owner can act as agent of the IBC, buying and selling assets and doing business on its behalf. Thus, assets are held under a corporate name, protecting the actual owner's privacy.

While IBCs were very popular in the 1970s and 1980s, the U.S. tax law has changed dramatically. These vehicles are not tax-free for Americans and now require a substantial amount of tax reporting. In certain situations, however, IBCs are still useful. In particular, they are useful for active international businesses

LLC or IBC?

While an IBC cannot conduct business in its country of incorporation, there is no such restriction on an LLC. And LLCs must file annual accounts. The members of an LLC are individually liable for taxes on their share of the profits if they are earned within the United States or if a member is a U.S. citizen or resident. For U.S. citizens, an offshore LLC is a better vehicle than an IBC because of simpler U.S. tax compliance.

that engage in trade, services, and so on. Also, in some situations, IBCs can be used to hold title to and transfer foreign real estate. However, IBCs should not be used for passive investments or passive income.

A Final Word: OAPT, Family Foundation, LLC, or IBC—Which One Is Best for Me?

As you can imagine, it's hard to offer individual solutions—especially in the confines of this book. Each one of you has different goals, unique situations, and your own ideas about what type of structures you prefer. To serve as basic guidelines, we have provided a summary of the benefits and limitations of each of the four entities we discussed in this chapter.

To learn which one is best for your particular situation, we suggest that you consult an experienced professional.

CHAPTER

4

OFFSHORE INVESTING: OFFSHORE STOCKS, BONDS, CURRENCIES, MUTUAL FUNDS, AND HEDGE FUNDS

I f you've ever traveled or visited a newsstand at the airport or in a local bookstore, you've probably seen a newspaper called the *Financial Times*. Inside its pinkish-colored pages, you'll find closing prices for stocks, government bonds, and currencies from far-off financial centers like Taiwan, Turkey, and Switzerland.

So why should you be interested in these faraway offshore markets? You may be scratching your head, asking yourself: "Doesn't the United States already have the largest stock market in the world?" Yes . . . it does. However, the U.S. stock market is shrinking compared to foreign markets as other economies grow faster, expand capital markets and become richer. And a big problem with the domestic investment options offered by Wall Street is that they are *all* denominated in U.S. dollars. Not to mention that some of the world's biggest profit opportunities today lie outside U.S. markets. Especially in a troubled market environment.

SEVEN REASONS WHY YOU SHOULD CONSIDER INVESTING OFFSHORE

1. Safer. Going offshore now is probably the most important investment decision confronting investors. That's because global banking diversification has never been more important with more than $1 trillion in write-downs tied to mortgage-backed securities and credit derivatives. European private banks, unlike money-center banks and commercial banks in the United States and elsewhere are far stronger and generally don't make mortgage loans or leveraged loans; these banks generate their revenues from wealth management, not gambling in derivatives. Despite the ongoing global turmoil, not a single Swiss bank has failed over the last 12 months.

2. Greater choice. The United States has the world's largest securities market, but if you're interested in other nations' currencies, stocks, bonds, and other assets, there is a much greater selection of investments offshore. For instance, there are more than 60,000 offshore funds

trading worldwide, but only about 11,000 located in the United States.

3. Higher returns. Many of those staid, safe investments from Wall Street simply don't produce the double- and triple-digit profits that are available offshore. In fact, the MSCI EAFE Index (the Europe, Australasia, and Far East Index, which consists of 1,000 stocks in 21 countries outside North and South America) beat out the S&P 500 from 2004 to mid-2008. Foreign markets really started to outpace U.S. stocks starting in 2004 (see Figure 4-1).

Figure 4-1 Foreign markets really started to outpace U.S. stocks starting in 2004.

4. Healthier economies abroad. Worldwide economic output surged nearly 52 percent from 2000 to 2007 thanks to the positive effects of globalization. And emerging markets like China, India, and Turkey are leading the pack of these healthy global performers (which also offer the best returns), while larger nations like the United States are slowing down. In fact, the United States accounts for only about 25 percent of the world's economy as measured by nominal GDP. This means that almost three-quarters of the world's economic output (i.e., the overwhelming majority) is generated outside of the United States. Certainly, the United States remains the world's largest economy by a wide margin; however, rapid economic growth rates elsewhere provide a reason to look beyond U.S. borders.

5. Stronger privacy. Investing offshore helps to secure your privacy by making it much more difficult for professional asset trackers, information brokers, and corporate espionage specialists to track your wealth. When you buy offshore investments through an offshore bank or insurance company, that institution acts as your nominee on the transaction and protects your confidentiality.

6. Hedge against sudden U.S. market risk. Access to global trading markets and foreign currencies in an account beyond your home borders will give you added protection should disaster strike. For five full days following the terrorist attack of September 11, 2001,

the U.S. markets were closed. When the markets finally reopened, the Dow had dropped 7 percent. Terrorism isn't the only risk—there are many other reasons why U.S. markets could shut down, such as a computer virus or a New York City–wide blackout. And, offshore, investors can tap into crisis investments like gold, silver, foreign government bonds and currencies—a prudent alternative to parking your money under the auspices of a bank in the United States where bankruptcies and bailouts continue to dominate the headlines. Storing a portion of your wealth offshore is therefore not only safe, but equally critical amid the worst economic crisis since the 1930s.

7. Potential currency profits. Anytime you purchase an offshore investment that's denominated in a foreign currency like the euro or the Japanese yen, you have the potential to earn additional profits if that currency rises against the U.S. dollar. For example, say you bought shares of Switzerland's largest bank, and your investment rose 13 percent over nine months in Swiss francs. Now suppose that the Swiss franc rose 4 percent against the U.S. dollar over that same time period. That means that you pocketed an additional gain of 4 percent—for a grand total of 17 percent—just because you bought an offshore stock denominated in a different currency.

Did you know that over the past 20 years, capital markets outside the United States have grown rapidly in size and importance? In 1970, non-U.S. stocks accounted for 34 percent of the world's $935 billion total market capitalization. (See Figure 4-2.)

But in 2008, U.S. stock markets represent less than a third of the world's total stock market capitalization of over $55 trillion. That means more than 67 percent of the world's total stock market capitalization is international, with the United States commanding less than 33 percent. The sad part of this story is that U.S. investors aren't taking full advantage of the rich profit potential in offshore markets. According to a recent survey, just 13 per-

Figure 4-2 Global stock market capitalization has now bypassed that of the U.S.

cent of Americans currently invest internationally, and only 19 percent plan to do so over the next five years.

That's incredible, considering the fact that international stocks have vastly outperformed the S&P 500 Index since 2003. As of this writing, the MSCI emerging market index fund was up a full 100 percent in that period . . . while the S&P gained nothing. That's right; zero.

And there are more than 1,500 emerging-markets investment funds alone, managing over $300 billion in equities. Add to that figure the billions more in exchange-traded funds, and you can see that there's a whole wide world of offshore investment opportunities that you should be taking full advantage of.

The ABCs of Offshore Investments

We are now going to outline the investment opportunities that exist offshore. While we won't be making specific investment recommendations, armed with knowledge of the various investments that are available offshore, you'll be able to decide what works best with your personal investment philosophy.

As a global investor, you can choose among various products and services, including

1. Global stocks: —the world is your oyster

2. Global bonds: —safety and diversification

3. Foreign currencies: —reap profits from currency fluctuations and currency markets

4. Global exchange-traded funds (ETFs) and mutual funds: —easy access to international and emerging markets

5. Global hedge funds: —an alternative investment for aggressive investors

6. Managed futures: —high risks but high rewards for aggressive investors

7. Global investment trusts: —the crème de la crème of equity funds

As we said in Chapter 2, your offshore bank account can offer you access to an incredible and endless variety of offshore investments, including mutual funds and index funds. Most private banks can purchase anything you want, assuming that the bank already maintains a relationship with that particular fund company. In some cases, the bank can still purchase funds outside of its dealing platform if the size of your transaction is more than $50,000. Just remember the tax issues with various investments if you are an American. More on that later.

Global Stocks: The World Is Your Oyster

From your offshore private bank, the world of offshore investments really can be your oyster. As long as you don't trade too frequently, your offshore bank account is a great platform for maximizing international opportunities in foreign currency–denominated equities.

Today, the majority of investment opportunities are found offshore, since international markets now make up two-thirds of global stock market capitalization. And these foreign stock markets are growing much faster than markets in the United States, offering greater total return potential. With an offshore private bank account, you can invest in almost any security, anywhere in the world, that's traded on a major exchange. This includes not just common stocks, but a growing list of foreign ETFs, too. What's also great about a foreign bank account is that it allows you to maximize the long-term benefits of international currency diversification.

It's no secret that the U.S. dollar has shed more than 72 percent of its value against the Swiss franc since 1971. The Swiss franc now trades just a few points above par value against the dollar. The U.S. dollar has also declined heavily against most other major currencies over the last 35 years, making currency diversification an essential long-term offshore financial planning requirement.

Did you know that during the 1930s, President Franklin D. Roosevelt got the U.S. Congress to pass laws that prevented U.S. residents from investing directly in foreign stocks, bonds, gold, and other funds? Even though these laws are no longer in effect, your stockbroker may be giving you the "run-around" when it comes to overseas investing. Don't believe it. You have the right to invest in any exchange-traded security in the *entire world*. Just abide by the tax laws affecting your holdings, gains and dividends, and the world is your playground. The saddest part of this denial of American freedom is that individuals like you have lost and continue to lose billions in profits. In recent years, offshore stock, bond, and currency markets have performed far better than U.S. exchanges.

Offshore Bonds: Safety and Diversification

Every single day, countries and companies around the world issue bonds to raise capital to finance economic expansion plans. It's a huge market that actually dwarfs the global stock market. Bonds are an obligation or promissory note from the issuing country or company. The issuer of a bond promises to pay the holder a fixed rate of interest periodically over time, until the bond reaches its maturity date, the date on which the issuer is obligated to pay you back your principal. Once the bond matures, you receive back the "par value" of the bond. Bonds generally have a par value of $1,000 (although government bonds usually have a higher amount) or the foreign currency par value in the country in which they are issued.

In 1982, bonds began their historical bull market after years of punishing inflation in the 1970s. Since then, fixed-income markets have logged some pretty eye-popping returns. Types of bonds include zero-coupon bonds, long-term bonds, emerging-market bonds, high-yield or junk bonds, and foreign currency bonds (bonds denominated in currencies other than U.S. dollars). Even Treasury bonds have posted some impressive profits over the last 25 years. Adjusted for rising inflation, these have averaged about 4 percent per year.

Like offshore stocks, offshore bonds are available in most major currencies around the world. That's what makes them so liquid. In fact, bonds denominated in foreign currencies provide the global market's best liquidity. And the currency market is the most liquid of all, with trillions of dollars traded daily. We'll tell you more about currencies in just a moment.

First, did you know you could invest in AAA-rated international bonds tax-free at the local level? The European Investment Bank (EIB) is the European Union's financing arm, similar to the U.S. Treasury. Each week, the EIB heads to global markets and raises a few hundred million dollars to finance its borrowing requirements. What's amazing about the EIB is its vast bond market universe. You can purchase EIB bonds denominated in euro, Swiss francs, British pounds sterling, Australian dollars, New Zealand dollars—you name it. And they're tax-free. Foreign, non-EU residents are paid income gross of withholding. Don't forget, though—you still have to declare the income to Uncle Sam!

Currencies Made Easy: Profit from Fluctuations

Many international investment opportunities present two benefits: access to true global markets and access to currency diversification. Rather than holding all of your investments in one currency, be it U.S. dollars, Canadian dollars, or euro, you have the option of mixing up your currency holdings.

In fact, currencies have been called "the ultimate asset class" because these markets can never experience an across-the-board bear market. If you choose wisely and invest at the right time, you can profit from currency appreciation on top of any increase the investment may have enjoyed. It's a win-win for you.

More Money, More Money—Thanks to Currencies

Keep in mind that when you buy stocks outside of your home country, you are also investing in the local currency, as we mentioned earlier.

And the currency return component of an offshore stock investment can either enhance or reduce the total return. Here's an example. Say you are a U.S.–based investor, and you invested in one of the world's largest commodities firms, BHP Billiton Ltd. BHP is an Australian company that's traded on the Australian stock exchange. When you originally bought the stock, BHP's stock was trading at around $15.76 Australian dollars (AUD) per share, and you bought 1,000 shares.

Here is how you would calculate your total return. Crunch the numbers, and you'll discover that you made an extra 16 percent just from the currency appreciation. To determine your U.S. dollar cost, just multiply the Australian dollar share price by the number of shares you purchased. Then multiply that number by the exchange rate between the Australian dollar and the U.S. dollar. You have two moving parts: the stock price and the exchange rate.

When you bought the stock, the AUD share price was $15.76. You bought 1,000 shares for $15,760 AUD. You paid: $15,760 AUD or $10,840 U.S. (the exchange rate then was 0.6867).

Now the share price is $26.70 AUD. Your 1,000 shares are now worth $26,700 AUD. The exchange rate is now 0.7515, so the shares worth $26,700 AUD are now worth $20,065 U.S.

Your U.S. dollar investment grew from $10,840 to $20,065, or 85 percent. The stock appreciation alone was 69.4 percent

($15.76 AUD/share to $26.70 AUD/share). But because you held stock denominated in Australian dollars, and the Australian dollar appreciated against the U.S. dollar while you held the stock, you made an extra 16 percent on top of the stock's appreciation.

There are hundreds of currencies across the globe. Here's a list of the ones you should know:

Majors:

U.S. dollar (USD)

Euro (EUR)

Japanese yen (JPY)

Swiss franc (CHF)

British pound (GBP)

Canadian dollar (CAD)

Australian dollar (AUD)

Others actively traded:

New Zealand dollar (NZD)

Swedish krona (SEK)

Norwegian krona (NOR)

Danish krone (DKK)

Singapore dollar (SGD)

South Korean won (KRW)

South African rand (ZAR)

Mexican peso (MXN)

Brazilian real (BRL)

Hong Kong dollar (HKD)

Major "managed" currency:

Chinese yuan (CNY)

How Does It All Work?

Currency prices are driven by many different variables, not the least of which is investor sentiment. This seems to make it all a bit difficult to understand. Currencies move and change prices based on a jumble of obscure relationships that are best left to the professionals to analyze.

However, there are a few key fundamental reasons why currencies move the way they do over the longer term. It's actually pretty easy to understand. Once you do, you will realize that currency investing fits very nicely into a global portfolio.

Two Major Factors That Drive Currencies

Every day a virtual frenzy of market data rolls across traders' computer screens. Some of those currency traders will use the data as an excuse to explain why a particular currency (like the good old greenback) moved up, down, or sideways. This flurry of data can include virtually anything in the markets, like trade deficits, oil prices, stock prices, industrial production, central bank pronouncements, geopolitical events, wheat prices, and even more.

While there is no single Holy Grail indicator to forecast currency moves, there are nevertheless two fundamental drivers. As a currency investor, you should keep an eye on the following areas:

1. *Differences in interest rates.* Generally speaking, money is attracted to the country or currency that offers the highest relative yield. This is why it's important to monitor global interest rates, and especially changes in those benchmark rates.

2. *Economic growth.* A healthy, fast-growing economy creates more investment opportunities, and therefore tends to attract more capital from around the world, which helps push up the value of the currency.

Another critically important factor that affects both interest rates and economic growth is market sentiment—that is, what are the expectations of currency market investors? That's the tricky part, and it explains why it's not always about interest rates, as many observers would have you believe. If it were, you would just have to scan the globe for the countries with the highest interest rate and then buy their currencies. Unfortunately, it's not quite that easy, but it can be rather simple if you know what you're doing.

It takes time and lots of real-world experience to take advantage of currency markets, but once you have a handle on market sentiment, you can start to predict how the market will respond to events—and make some nice profits from this new-found wisdom.

Diversification and the Big Swing

Okay, you now have an understanding of the fundamentals that move currencies. Let's take a brief look at why you might consider adding currencies to your global portfolio. (See Figure 4-3.)

First, currencies cut down on the risk in your portfolio, because they are not correlated with stocks and bonds. That means that even if the global markets correct all around the world, certain currencies will still rally.

Second, currencies often move in multiyear trends. If you can catch even a part of the trend and remain committed to it, you can make a lot of money. And as Wall Street legend Jesse Livermore said: "The big money is in the big swing."

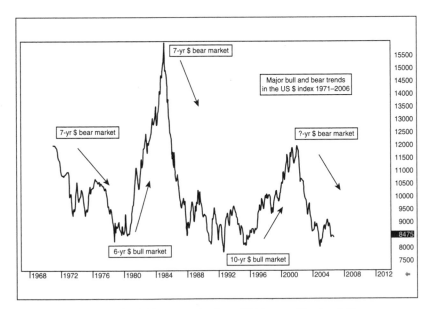

Figure 4-3 The U.S. Dollar over the Last 30 Years—Plenty of Chances to Ride the Trends.

Four Different Ways to Take Advantage of the Currency Markets

When you are investing and trading in currencies, you have lots of investment options. If you're interested in trading currencies, the first thing you need to do is make a few key decisions. Ask yourself, how much risk do you want to use? What kind of profits are you looking for? What kind of holding periods do you feel most comfortable with (short-term or long-term)? What is the purpose of the investment . . . is it for retirement savings or pure speculation?

Once you've completed your self-analysis, you need to choose the best way to access the currency market that also fits your investment comfort zone. Here are your choices, listed by risk level (low to high):

1. *Multiple-currency deposits (bank account).* This is a flexible and safe way to diversify your risk outside of your home currency and achieve a respectable yield while protecting the purchasing power of your cash.

   You can park your cash in a bank account and denominate your cash in any currency you choose. Or, you can keep your cash in many different currencies. All you need is a bank account that offers multiple-currency deposits.

2. *Currency exchange-traded funds (ETFs).* In 2006, currency ETFs were launched on the market, opening the world of currency trading to everyone who has a standard stock brokerage account. Currency ETFs allow you to jump

aboard a hot currency trend and then hold your ETF for as long (or as short) as you like. Just like a stock.

When we first started working on this book about two years ago, only eight currency ETFs were available. Now, there are many ETFs available on the market—offering both the majors and what we like to call the exotics:

CurrencyShares Australian Dollar Trust ETF (FXA)

CurrencyShares British Pound Sterling Trust ETF (FXB)

CurrencyShares Canadian Dollar Trust ETF (FXC)

CurrencyShares Euro Trust ETF (FXE)

CurrencyShares Japanese Yen Trust ETF (FXY)

CurrencyShares Mexican Peso Trust ETF (FXM)

CurrencyShares Swedish Krona Trust ETF (FXS)

CurrencyShares Swiss Franc Trust ETF (FXF)

ELEMENTS Australian Dollar/U.S. Dollar Exchange Rate ETN (ADE)

ELEMENTS British Pound/U.S. Dollar Exchange Rate ETN (EGB)

ELEMENTS Euro/U.S. Dollar Exchange Rate ETN (ERE)

ELEMENTS U.S. Dollar/Canadian Dollar Exchange Rate ETN (CUD)

ELEMENTS U.S. Dollar/Swiss Franc Exchange Rate ETN (SZE)

EUR/USD Exchange Rate ETN (ERO)

GBP/USD Exchange Rate ETN (GBB)

iPath Optimized Currency Carry ETN (ICI)

JPY/USD Exchange Rate ETN (JYN)

Market Vectors Chinese Renminbi/USD ETN (CNY)

Market Vectors Double Long Euro ETN (URR)

Market Vectors Double Short Euro ETN (DRR)

Market Vectors Indian Rupee/USD ETN (INR)

PowerShares DB G10 Currency Harvest Fund (DBV)

PowerShares DB U.S. Dollar Index Bearish Fund (UDN)

WisdomTree Dreyfus Brazilian Real Fund (BZF)

WisdomTree Dreyfus Chinese Yuan Fund (CYB)

WisdomTree Dreyfus Emerging Currency Fund–Active (CEW)

WisdomTree Dreyfus Euro Fund (EU)

WisdomTree Dreyfus Indian Rupee Fund (ICN)

WisdomTree Dreyfus Japanese Yen Fund (JYF)

WisdomTree Dreyfus New Zealand Dollar Fund (BNZ)

WisdomTree Dreyfus South African Rand Fund (SZR)

WisdomTree U.S. Current Income Fund (USY)

Currency ETFs offer five key advantages: they're low in cost, easily accessible, efficiently priced, and have constant liquidity. Plus, ETFs offer nearly unlimited investment strategies.

3. *Currency options.* Currency options are another effective and easy way to play the currency markets.

Currency options offer many key benefits. For starters, you can trade these options with your typical stock options account. You don't need a special platform or broker to participate. Your risk is limited to the amount of the premium you pay per option (assuming that you only buy calls or puts as the opening transaction), plus your brokerage commission. And options are highly leveraged, so your profits can be huge if you pick a winning trade.

Options could be for you if you like to speculate in the markets, shoot for big profits with limited risk, and don't want to sit in front of a trading screen all day. Currency options also offer intermediate-term trading opportunities based on global economic themes that affect currencies.

4. *Currency futures and spot forex.* While special accounts and trading platforms are required to participate in the futures and spot forex markets, this is where you can produce big-time returns in a very short period of time. But you also take on higher risk because you use leverage to get those bigger returns. Winning in futures and spot forex requires not only good analysis, but extremely disciplined risk control. And positions move fast, so you have to stay connected and highly focused. It's not unusual to enter and exit a trade in the same day.

So there's a lot of potential for big profits, but you have to be disciplined.

Offshore Mutual Funds: VIP Access to Global Equities and Emerging Markets

Offshore mutual funds are household names in the investment management business. They operate under securities laws very similar to those in the United States. In some cases, securities laws are even stricter in the European Union (EU). Overall, mutual funds sold through private banks are generally reputable and credible products.

The biggest advantage offered by these offshore funds, and also by a growing number of ETFs, is access to international and especially emerging markets, which historically, have absolutely blown away domestic markets in terms of performance.

As you can see in Figure 4-4, international equity markets have outperformed the U.S. market by between 30 and 100 percent since 2003. Emerging markets alone have returned 100 percent in that period, while the S&P actually suffered a loss.

Mutual funds and ETFs offer the easiest ways to tap into offshore markets, but hedge funds are very different animals. Since most of us are familiar with mutual funds, we'll start here.

A mutual fund is a collective investment company that pools resources from the public to make investments. Mutual funds are structured as either open- or closed-end funds and may sell at net asset value or at a discount to their net asset value, depending on how the company is structured.

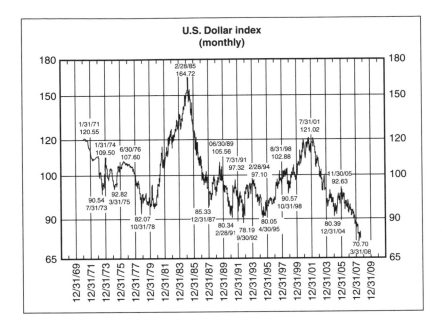

Figure 4-4 The U.S. Dollar over the Last 30 Years—Plenty of Chances to Ride the Trends.

Why Most Americans Never Hear About Offshore Mutual Funds

The U.S. Securities and Exchange Commission prohibits offshore or non-U.S.-registered funds from soliciting U.S. investors. In theory, this is to protect U.S. investors from unscrupulous and unregulated investments. Overseas, the regulations and requirements for mutual funds vary across all jurisdictions from a highly regulated environment to none at all.

And even though we believe there are a number of very good offshore fund companies out there that aren't registered with the SEC, many simply do not want to be bothered with all of the paperwork and filing requirements of the SEC, not to mention the IRS, just so they can market their funds in the United States . . .

Today, mutual funds are where you'll find all the great managers specializing in stocks and, to a lesser extent, bonds. In fact, some of the greatest money managers have captained open-end mutual funds over the last 100 years, including Philip Carret, Peter Lynch, Ken Heebner, Bill Gross, and Mario Gabelli. Mutual funds are bought and sold on a daily basis Monday through Friday. They invest in a very wide spectrum of global investment opportunities, mostly equities and fixed-income investments. Offshore, the average annual total expense ratio, or cost for owning a mutual fund, is 2 percent per annum. That's high by U.S. standards. In the United States, the average mutual fund charges 1.7 percent per annum in fees.

Currencies also play a big role in global investment portfolios. The great advantage of offshore funds compared to U.S. funds is that virtually all products are offered not only in U.S. dollars, but also in euro, another strong currency since its introduction in 1999. Since the euro was adopted, the mutual fund industry has thrived in Europe, and dollar- and euro-denominated mutual funds are now widely sold.

Why Aren't All Funds Registered in the United States?

One of the main obstacles for non-U.S. fund managers is that the United States requires that any investment sold in the United States must be registered not only with the SEC, but also with similar agencies in each of the 50 states. As you can imagine, this is a very labor-intensive and expensive process.

In addition, the United States requires far more securities disclosure than most countries, and U.S. accounting practices differ from those in Europe and other areas. Ironically, to avoid SEC red tape and registration costs, U.S. citizens run several leading mutual and hedge funds with excellent performance records, but will only accept accredited U.S. investors (those with a net worth of $1 million or more) or foreigners.

The opportunities really are endless, including the most popular for getting started: global equity funds, or funds that invest mostly in major-economy stock markets like those of the United States, Western Europe, and Japan. Other widely offered sectors include regional equities (Asia, Latin America) and sector funds (health care, technology). There are also real estate funds in Europe, Eastern Europe, Asia, and Latin America (real estate investment trusts), bonds (government and high-yield), single-country funds (Germany, Thailand, and Brazil), and emerging-market stocks and fixed-income securities. Today you have more than 80,000 collective investment companies to choose from. Most of these are open-end mutual funds; there are fewer closed-end funds.

In some cases, offshore funds and investments are available only to accredited investors. This is a designation created by the SEC. To qualify as an accredited investor, you must have a net worth of $1 million or more or an annual income of at least $200,000 per year for each of the last two years. In other words, "Ya gotta have a lotta money."

If you are an accredited investor, you have a freer hand to buy non-SEC-registered foreign stocks, mutual funds, and hedge funds directly. Recently, the SEC proposed changing this rule and upping the ante by including a new qualification: an investor must own at least $2.5 million in investments to be considered accredited. In addition, the $2.5 million test will be periodically adjusted for inflation.

Exchange-Traded Funds: the Best of Both Worlds for Global Investors

A relatively new investment product is quickly becoming the investment of choice for today's global investor. Exchange-traded funds (ETFs) are perhaps the most innovative product introduced since the advent of mutual funds more than a half-century ago.

First introduced in 1993, ETFs offer many of the advantages of mutual funds, including diversification and access to overseas markets, but they trade like common stocks and are listed on global exchanges. Today, there is almost $500 billion in ETF assets listed in the United States, plus hundreds of millions worth of ETFs traded in Europe, Canada, Japan, Hong Kong, and many other foreign exchanges.

ETFs are soaring in popularity thanks to several significant advantages that they enjoy over both traditional mutual funds and individual securities:

- *Instant diversification and full transparency.* As you've probably been told many times, diversification is important to your investment portfolio because it tends to lower your risk. Most ETFs are designed to track broad market indexes or sectors. As a result, ETFs typically hold anywhere from a few dozen up to several hundred separate securities. So you benefit by gaining instant diversification in just one single transaction.

  Also, a diversified ETF is often much less risky and volatile than individual securities, where you must always be concerned about company-, sector-, or country-specific headline risks that can have a negative impact on individual positions.

- *Trading flexibility.* ETFs span virtually every asset class available to investors: stocks, bonds (both foreign and domestic), value stocks, growth stocks, small-cap, large-cap, individual sectors and industry groups, corporate bonds, government bonds, foreign currencies, commodities, real estate—you name it.

  ETFs also offer instant liquidity because they trade throughout the day during market hours, whereas open-end mutual funds are priced only at the end of the day.

ETFs are also fully transparent in that all securities held by an ETF are reported each trading day. This key feature lets you know exactly what you will own when you are considering an ETF for purchase.

Finally, unlike mutual funds, ETFs can also be sold short in hopes of capitalizing on a falling market or weakness in a particular sector. And they can be purchased on margin, to leverage your upside potential. All of these features offer you more flexibility as an investor.

- *Lower-cost investments.* The expense ratios of ETFs are considerably lower than those of actively managed mutual funds. According to data from Morningstar, the average expense ratio of traditional mutual funds is 1.67 percent of assets yearly, while ETF expense ratios are just 0.44 percent on average.

   ETFs have no front-end or deferred sales charges (or loads); instead, as with individual stocks, you pay only standard commissions when you buy and sell ETFs.

- *Tax efficiency.* According to a recent Morningstar report, ETFs have proved to be much more tax-efficient than the typical mutual fund. The reason is the unique way ETFs are structured, resulting in little, if any, taxable capital gain distributions to shareholders at year end.

The bottom line is that ETFs track most of the same market or sector indexes that mutual funds do, and also give you access to most major offshore markets and alternative investments like currencies and commodities, and yet ETFs are available for lower cost.

Hedge Funds: An Alternative Investment

In addition to ETFs and mutual funds, you can also buy hedge funds, either domestically or offshore. Hedge funds are technically managed futures funds and are known in the asset management world as "alternative investments." These funds are considered the "Rolls Royce" of investment vehicles, but they come with many warnings.

Hedge funds come in all shapes and sizes, with different risk parameters. It's estimated that more than 15,000 hedge funds are currently in business, with industry assets now estimated at around $3 trillion worldwide. A hedge fund is structured in a manner similar to a mutual fund in that it involves collectively pooling assets under the supervision of a professional money manager or a team of asset managers.

However, this is where the similarities end. Rather than being SEC-registered investment companies, most hedge funds are structured as partnerships/joint ventures, limited liability companies (LLCs), or limited partnerships (LPs). Hedge funds are also much riskier than mutual funds. For starters, hedge fund managers typically use leverage to boost their returns, whereas traditional mutual fund managers don't.

Hedge funds are very illiquid investments. You typically need to give at least 30 days' notice to redeem shares at the end of a month or a quarter. Hedge funds in the United States are not governed by the same U.S. regulations as mutual funds. Hedge funds charge very steep fees. In comparison, mutual funds just charge a management fee, but hedge funds levy a management fee (usually 1 to 2 percent of assets) *and* a performance fee of 15 to 20 percent of net profits.

If you're interested in hedge funds, you may want to look offshore. Unlike hedge funds sold in the United States, which are available only to accredited investors, offshore hedge funds are available to the retail public, starting as low as a $25,000 investment, but minimums generally average about $250,000. A word of caution: hedge fund risks can reward you with significant profits. But with the high fees and high risks, you should plan to limit your portfolio's exposure to these alternative investments.

Managed Futures: High Risk and High Reward

Managed futures are another form of alternative investment available to aggressive investors. Like hedge funds, these products use leverage to increase total returns. Managed futures funds are also known as commodity trading advisors, or CTAs. These are heavily regulated in the United States, but not strictly monitored offshore.

Futures traders are a very aggressive breed of asset managers. They use tons of leverage and margin to trade global futures and options contracts, long and short. Historically, these funds have earned big profits during bear markets—especially during the 2000–2002 bear market. But for most investors, this asset class is too speculative, illiquid, and very expensive. Managed futures typically levy a fat 5 percent management fee, or more, and charge a performance fee of 15 percent of net profits. However, there is one bright spot: if there are no profits, no fee is charged.

Investment Trusts: The *Crème de la Crème* of Equity Funds

The first collective investment vehicle dates way back to Scotland in 1865. Called "investment trusts," these funds are structured almost identically to closed-end funds in the United States. This "crème de la crème" of equity funds could be the aggressive part of your global investment portfolio that you are seeking.

Along with their great performance over the last 141 years, U.K. investment trusts offer a wide selection of other advantages. For starters, they have established global growth equity and sector equity opportunities. Historically, they have also posted some very impressive returns. And if you set up your investment trust in the United Kingdom, you get an extra currency "kicker" from the generally rock-solid British pound.

Investment trusts traded on the London Stock Exchange (LSE) also usually trade at a discount to their net asset value (NAV). That's rule 1 for investment trusts: always buy them at a discount and never at a premium to their NAV, or more than they're worth.

It's always best to buy below cost, buy good management, and let the stock market realize the discount or book value of the investment. Incidentally, book value means your net assets, after expenses, liabilities, and other obligations to the company. Assuming that you buy the right funds with great long-term track records, investment trusts belong in a diversified global portfolio.

Remember to keep very aggressive funds, like investment trusts and hedge funds, limited to a small portion of your total portfolio.

WHAT TO KNOW BEFORE YOU INVEST: TAXES AND OFFSHORE INVESTMENTS

Before you dive into the different types of offshore investments on your own, let's take a moment to review the tax issues involved with investing offshore. While we have devoted an entire chapter (Chapter 6) to taxes and reporting, it's important that we address taxes briefly in this section. Before you send a penny offshore, the first thing you should do is make sure that you fully understand the tax consequences of trading and investing abroad.

This is also the time to carefully strategize about what you want to achieve from your offshore portfolio. Are you looking to invest only in offshore mutual funds, or do you want to invest in international stocks traded on various exchanges? Maybe you're seeking a place to park a basket of cash in international currencies or gold to hedge against the long-term decline of the U.S. dollar. Regardless of your personal goals, make sure that you fully understand how these investments will be taxed by the IRS (or your home country) before you buy anything.

The Secret to Investing in Offshore Mutual Funds

We have to point out that, since 1986, the United States has changed the way offshore mutual funds are taxed. Unless they are held in a tax-deferred account such as a variable annuity or offshore IRA account, offshore mutual funds are effectively taxed each year by the IRS, even though most offshore funds do *not* make year-end distributions.

In the United States, mutual funds typically issue year-end dividends, capital gains, and other income distributions to shareholders. That's not the case offshore. Offshore funds don't report their share of income or gains to investors. That means that if you buy an offshore fund outside of a tax-deferred vehicle, you'll be liable for taxes on this source of income each year, even if the off-shore funds in your portfolio didn't make a single distribution all year long. And the taxes are quite onerous.

Foreign investment funds are treated under the Internal Revenue Code as "passive foreign investment companies" (PFICs). Technically speaking, a PFIC is any foreign company that derives at least 75 percent of its gross income from passive activities or that derives passive income from at least 50 percent of its assets. Nearly all of the income of an investment fund is passive income. So, nearly all offshore funds are PFICs for U.S. shareholders. This creates an unfavorable tax situation for Americans.

So, how are PFICs taxed? There are three options to choose from:

Section 1291 Fund Excess Distributions Method. This is the default method (i.e., the method used unless one of the alternatives is selected). All income and gains are taxed at the highest ordinary income rate. There is no long-term capital gains treatment. Losses are not allowed. Finally, you have to assume that all of the gains are earned equally over the time the investment was held—even if the fund lost money the first few years and only made its gains in the last year when you cashed out. Why is that bad? Interest charges, compounded annually. Annually compounded interest at the underpayment interest rate (which is set by the Treasury Department each quarter and has been anywhere from 5 to 10 percent over the last several years) is charged on deferred tax.

Mark-to-Market Method. The mark-to-market method allows an owner of PFIC shares to mark gains to market at each year end. In other words, you pay tax on the difference between the fair market value of the shares at the beginning of the year and the fair market value of the shares at the end of the year, and you start fresh each January 1st. Gains and losses are all ordinary, not capital.

Qualified Electing Fund Method. If a fund meets certain accounting and reporting requirements, a shareholder can elect to treat the fund as a Qualified Electing Fund (QEF). The effect is that the offshore fund shares are taxed like U.S. shares. In addition, a QEF shareholder can elect to defer tax on undistributed fund income, paying the tax (plus interest at the underpayment rate) when the income is actually distributed. Few U.S. investors make QEF elections for offshore fund shares because it is impossible to do so in most cases. Offshore funds, even those that are essentially offshore clones of U.S. funds, simply do not keep U.S. books and tax records and provide U.S. tax information to their shareholders, which is a requirement for making the QEF election.

So remember, if you're considering tapping into offshore funds, purchase these securities through a tax-deferred structure. We explain these tax-deferred options in Chapter 5. Investing in international stocks, bonds, and currencies using an offshore bank or an offshore LLC is certainly less taxing than investing in offshore mutual funds.

In a nutshell, capital gains on international stocks are taxed the same as gains on stocks traded domestically in the United States. The only caveat is that stocks held in a non-U.S. bank are subject to a withholding tax on dividends, if any are paid. However, you can obtain a dividend tax credit in the United States if the country where you invested has a tax treaty with your home country. (See Chapter 6.)

How a Tax Treaty Works to Avoid Double Taxation

Marc has an offshore bank account in Switzerland. He decides to purchase shares of Nestlé denominated in Swiss francs (CHF). At the end of the year, he receives a dividend payment of 100 CHF from Nestlé. However, Marc doesn't receive 100 CHF; he receives 75 CHF, and his bank withholds the remaining 25 CHF. When it's time for Marc to file his U.S. taxes, he can claim the 25 CHF on his U.S. tax form, but he'll have to produce his Swiss banking statement, which will show both the dividend payment and the withheld tax.

International Bonds

The United States does not levy any penalties on income distributions on international bonds. The local bank where you hold the bonds will not withhold income, although the burden is on you to report the income distribution to the IRS every year.

Currencies

As for currencies, any capital appreciation on foreign-exchange gains must be reported to the IRS. There are no punitive tax consequences on foreign currency capital gains derived from non-U.S. banks. Income derived from currency deposits or CDs, however, must be reported to the IRS as well.

A FINAL WORD ON OFFSHORE INVESTING

As you can see, there are many investment products you can choose from when you decide to invest offshore. So take your time and figure out which investments are right for you and your portfolio. And while you're weighing your options, check with a local tax attorney to make sure you won't face any negative tax consequences when you do go offshore.

Remember, you want to be ready just in case the U.S. dollar takes another dive. And any one of these offshore investment ideas can help with your overall goal—to diversify part of your wealth away from the sinking U.S. dollar. Especially today, in the midst of the worst credit crisis and stock market collapse in more than a generation, it's time to move some of your hard-earned assets offshore to safer shores.

So get going! You'll be glad you did when you start seeing bigger profits show up in your portfolio.

OFFSHORE ONE-STOP SOLUTIONS: VARIABLE ANNUITIES, LIFE INSURANCE, AND RETIREMENT PLANS

In this chapter, we'll introduce what we call offshore "one-stop solutions": offshore annuities, life insurance, and retirement plans. We call them one-stop solutions because with just one of them, you can achieve several of your wealth objectives:

- Asset protection
- Privacy
- Investment and currency diversification
- Tax deferral

- Access to global investments that aren't available to Americans

- Estate planning (apart from your ordinary estate)

There's a good chance that you already have a U.S. or domestic version of one of these structures in your financial plan. For reasons that you'll see in a moment, establishing or moving these structures offshore could maximize your opportunity for profit, diversification, asset protection, and privacy potential with each of the structures. You might be tempted to skip over this chapter. Let's face it: what more do you need to know about insurance or annuities—or IRAs, for that matter? They're safe. They're boring.

Well, give us 20 minutes and we'll show you the sexier side of these offshore best buys.

A Crash Course in Annuities

You won't find any surprises here. While the term *annuity* encompasses many types of income arrangements, it is most often used to describe the situation in which an insurance company agrees to make a series of payments to someone for the rest of his life in exchange for a single premium. However, much like a trust or foundation (see Chapter 3), offshore annuities can also act as a unique holding structure for your assets.

Since offshore fixed annuities don't really offer much more benefit than their onshore cousins, we'll focus primarily on offshore variable annuities.

Variable Annuities—Not Your Typical Insurance Policy

In response to consumer demand for more lucrative investment returns from their annuity contracts, many insurance companies developed "variable-return" annuity policies, where some or all of the funds on deposit are invested in stocks or other securities.

With this arrangement, the investment income earned by the insurance company will vary depending on the performance of the underlying investments for as long as the annuity is in force.

A *variable annuity* is an insurance contract in which the insurance company guarantees a minimum payment at the end of the cash accumulation stage. The remaining income payments can vary depending on the performance of a managed investment portfolio. The portfolio can be invested in a variety of ways and its performance determines the amount of the eventual total annuity payment.

It works as follows: you buy a variable annuity contract (policy) for an agreed-upon sum, often referred to as a "single premium," though you can add to the policy as often as you wish. The insurance company invests these monies in accordance with one or more investment strategies that you approve. (We'll dig deeper into the investment opportunities available in just a moment.) The gains from those investments are compounded and are tax-deferred until you start receiving payouts, at which time the payout is taxed as regular income.

This tax-deferred accumulation can continue until the contract maturity date, which, for tax reasons, can be any time after age 59^1/$_2$—also a time when your total income is lower because you have retired and your income tax bracket is lower.

Setting up an offshore annuity is beneficial because with this one unique holding structure, you can secure

1. *Nearly any investment you can imagine.* This includes stocks, bonds, currencies, investment portfolios, and even those forbidden offshore funds we told you about in Chapter 4.

2. *Enhanced asset protection* from creditors, lawsuits, greedy partners, and ex-spouses.

3. *Speedy estate planning.* Your assets go right to your beneficiaries upon your death, bypassing probate.

4. *Tax-deferred growth.* If a policy is structured correctly, it allows your funds to grow tax-deferred.

5. *Currency diversification.* Foreign insurance companies frequently permit premium payments, withdrawals, borrowings, and death benefits in different currencies.

6. *Greater flexibility.* These policies can be adjusted as needed, and they can also be transferred to and combined with other legal structures that you may want to set up later.

Your Gateway to Once-Forbidden Offshore Investments

Industry insiders often suggest that an offshore variable annuity be used as a gateway to going offshore, since it offers a variety of financial benefits rolled up into one structure. Offshore variable annuities are one of the easiest, least expensive methods of investing in those lucrative offshore funds that we told you about in Chapter 4. These are the ones that are typically restricted for U.S. investors, yet often outperform the U.S. indexes.

Most companies that offer variable annuities provide a range of investments that are not guaranteed products. Their performance is variable, meaning that they are tied to the securities that the annuity's asset manager selects. Most often, these securities include global equities, foreign currencies, bonds, commodities, and sometimes even alternative investments like hedge funds and managed futures funds. These products are suited for the long-term investor looking for income at retirement with an investment horizon of at least five years, and preferably longer.

So what does this mean for you? Here's the exciting answer: complete and unfettered access to those lucrative offshore funds!

Now They Are Even More Powerful

In recent years, some insurance companies have developed annuity contracts with highly innovative features. One popular option is to permit the annuity owner (that's you) to request that a specific investment manager manage part or all of the assets in the portfolio. This request must be nonbinding for purposes of compliance with IRS regulations. This being said, you are not allowed to self-direct the investments. All investments must be selected by an investment manager approved by the insurance company.

The IRS has published investment and diversification guidelines for variable annuities. The guidelines dictate how the assets within the policy must be diversified. Failure to meet these guidelines means that the contract cannot constitute an annuity for tax purposes.

In order for an annuity to qualify for tax purposes, it must adhere to these guidelines:

1. No more than 55 percent of the value of the account's total assets may be represented by any one investment.

2. No more than 70 percent may be represented by two investments, 80 percent by three investments, or 90 percent by four investments.

Therefore, you should be certain that the policy is fully compliant with current U.S. tax rules. In addition, if you opt for having an investment manager manage the assets in the annuity, that manager must be educated on the issue and carefully monitored to assure compliance with the rules.

One of the Last Vestiges of Tax Deferral

Variable annuity policies, both domestic and offshore, keep growing over the long term, tax-free, until you "annuitize" them (i.e., you begin taking income from them). They remain one of the last vestiges of tax-deferred compounding for U.S. investors who are seeking a first-class portfolio of top-performing offshore money managers. Investors don't have to pay any annual taxes on the growth of the investments within an offshore variable annuity—the gains are tax-deferred until the policy is cashed out or annuity payments begin.

> ### Tax Tip
>
> One of the major disadvantages of an annuity contract is that income from the annuity is taxed as ordinary income, not as a long-term capital gain or qualified dividend. So instead of paying the 15 percent tax rate set for long-term capital gains or qualified dividends, you could pay up to 35 percent in federal tax plus whatever state tax, if any, applies where you live.

Variable annuities are usually liquid, in case you need access to cash before you are eligible to begin receiving payments. You can take out partial withdrawals or income payments without paying any penalties—even after the first day. However, you will have to pay income tax on any growth from the investments in the policy, but not on the original premium paid to the insurance company.

When you begin receiving payments from a variable annuity, that cash is taxed at ordinary U.S. income tax rates—up to 35 percent plus any applicable state taxes. A loan against a variable annuity from the issuing insurance company to the annuity owner is also considered by the IRS to be taxable income. However, borrowing against an annuity when it is first purchased is not taxable, because at that point no deferred income has accumulated.

Tax Tip

Section 72 of the U.S. Internal Revenue Code treats both foreign and domestic variable annuities the same way. But an offshore insurance company must follow the IRS rules in order for accumulations to qualify for tax deferral. Always obtain legal opinions on the U.S. tax treatment of annuities issued by a particular insurance company. Check with tax advisors if you are in doubt.

An Impenetrable Fortress

An offshore variable annuity policy is also a nearly impenetrable asset protection tool. If these policies are properly structured and established in the right jurisdiction, they cannot be seized or included in any bankruptcy proceeding 12 months after the setup of the policy. These rock-solid asset protection vehicles are also easy to establish. The owner also keeps full control, except, as we've noted, over the specific investments made in the annuity portfolio. Although domestic annuity contracts are not recorded or registered in any government database that is open to the public, the policyholder and beneficiary information is included in the database of the insurance company. There are few restrictions on how the insurance company may use that information.

In contrast, even if the existence of an offshore annuity contract is disclosed during a deposition or by court order, most offshore insurance companies will not disclose any details about the policy to any U.S. creditor or in response to any order by any U.S.

-court. An exception may apply if the applicable country has a treaty with the United States permitting an exchange of information, but this exception will not apply with respect to civil litigation or nongovernment creditors.

How an Annuity Can Save You When Disaster Strikes!

An annuity professional we know in Zurich told us these real-life stories:

- *The Floridian CPA.* In the early 1990s, a certified public accountant (CPA) from Florida came to our friend's Zurich office and purchased a Swiss annuity policy. At that time, this CPA was very successful in his business, and he advised only the wealthiest clients. In 1995, the CPA decided to retire, but he kept advising some of his largest and most affluent clients.

  But disaster struck in the late 1990s. The CPA gave one of his clients the wrong advice. Unfortunately, it seems that the CPA had *not* kept up with the legal changes affecting his profession after his retirement (so giving the wrong advice was entirely his fault).

  The CPA's client took him to court, and the retired CPA lost his assets in the suit that followed.

  Of course, his creditors also tried to seize his offshore annuity. We say tried because they tried and failed to liquidate his policy and seize the assets. His assets remained safely housed in his annuity policy.

To this day, the Floridian CPA lives off the income from his intact Swiss annuity policy.

• *The Canadian hotel owner.* This client was a wealthy woman who owned several hotels. Unfortunately, at a certain point, her business turned sour, and she had to file for bankruptcy. The Canadian judge decided that her Swiss annuity was part of the bankruptcy estate. So the Swiss insurer was informed of this and asked to liquidate the policy immediately.

Even though the request was appropriately presented, the Swiss insurer did not divulge any information. The insurance company fully protected the hotel owner's privacy and responded to inquiries only in generic form. The creditors were informed that the insurer was not allowed to give out any information to third parties.

The insurance company wouldn't even say that a woman bearing this name was a client of the insurance company! Furthermore, the insurer told the creditors that in the event of bankruptcy (of a policy owner), Swiss law fully protects the policy because ownership was transferred to the beneficiaries automatically, as documented in the accord. Any instructions subsequently forced upon the original policy owner could no longer be recognized. Only her beneficiaries, as the new owners of the policy, could give instructions to the insurance company.

Where in the World Should You Set Up an Annuity?

1. Liechtenstein
2. Isle of Man
3. The Cayman Islands
4. Bermuda

See Chapter 8 for more information about these havens.

Tip

If you have a variable annuity in the United States, you can transfer it offshore without paying taxes or penalties via a 1035 exchange. This is not to be confused with a 1031 exchange, which is used mostly for real estate and business assets.

What Does It Cost to Set Up an Annuity?

A foreign annuity can be obtained for as little as $100,000, and the ongoing expenses can come to about 2 percent of the assets in the contract (1 percent for administrative costs, 1 percent for asset management). There may also be a front-end load as high as 6 percent. However, if this load is charged, it is generally payable over an extended period—typically five years, or 1.2 percent per year. The initial expenses are those incurred to travel to a foreign country to actually purchase the contract. Note that many foreign insurance companies require the insured to sign the documents and make the premium payments outside of the United States.

At first glance, offshore policies may look a little more expensive than U.S. policies. They aren't. Offshore companies tend to disclose all the fees up front, so that you know what you can expect to pay. U.S. insurance companies are masters at hiding fees, especially if you choose to surrender. Also, the fees you pay depend upon the amounts you wish to invest. Fees can be substantially reduced for larger policies. Many Americans expect a cheap solution. Offshore policies are not cheap, but they provide an excellent value for the price.

OFFSHORE LIFE INSURANCE — LEGALLY AVOID ALL ESTATE TAXES

Despite all the talk of "estate tax reform" in the United States, without proper estate planning, the combination of income tax and estate tax can consume 80 percent or more of your entire estate at your death. Life insurance protects against the income loss that results if the insured dies. The named beneficiary receives the proceeds and thus avoids the financial impact of the death of the insured. The goal of life insurance is to provide financial security for your family after you die.

You can avoid these ruinous U.S. death taxes with several planning techniques, but only variable life insurance provides four key benefits:

1. Tax-free buildup of cash value, including dividends, interest, and capital gains.

2. Tax-free borrowing against cash value through policy loans—you can access as much as 90 percent of the invested funds without paying tax or interest.

3. Tax-free receipt of the death benefit.

4. Freedom from all estate taxes with special structuring.

These benefits are available with any life insurance policy that complies with U.S. tax laws. For larger estates, a U.S. tax-compliant life insurance policy issued by an offshore insurance carrier outside the United States offers five additional benefits:

1. *Increased asset protection.* This is like having an iron curtain around your wealth. Back home in the United States, there is no protection for life insurance proceeds under federal laws. While many states have laws that provide limited protection for life insurance policies, coverage varies from significant to nonexistent. In contrast, many offshore jurisdictions provide statutory asset protection for the death benefit and investments held by an insurance policy. For practical purposes, it is much more expensive for a creditor to bring a claim against a life insurance policy in a foreign court than in a domestic court.

Where in the World Should You Invest in an Offshore Life Insurance Policy?

1. Isle of Man

2. Switzerland

3. Bermuda

4. The Cayman Islands

5. Guernsey

For more information on these havens, see Chapter 8.

2. *Access to global investments.* Much like offshore variable annuities, offshore life insurance policies provide tax-advantaged access to international asset managers and to offshore funds that, as you now know, are blocked for most U.S. investors. You can be your own Warren Buffett.

3. *Minimum reporting requirements.* There are no requirements in the Internal Revenue Code that explicitly require that the existence of an offshore variable annuity or life insurance policy contract be disclosed to the IRS. This has led some tax advisors to state that they need not be reported as a "foreign bank, securities or 'other' financial account" (see Chapter 6). However, offshore annuity or insurance contracts that contain securities arguably constitute an "offshore securities account" and thus *are* reportable. The conservative stance is to report the existence of such contracts if they contain securities (which they nearly always do). If you're not sure, talk to a qualified tax advisor.

4. *Greater currency diversification.* Say good-bye to the unstable U.S. dollar. Offshore variable annuities and life insurance policies are free to make investments in any currency in the world, and many of these currencies will appreciate in value as the U.S. dollar fluctuates.

5. *Quick and easy offshore asset distribution.* An offshore insurance policy can arrange your estate in such a way that your international assets, such as offshore bank accounts, are easily passed onto your heirs. The policy can help avoid long waiting periods and probate allowing your beneficiaries access to the money much faster.

To ensure that your policy is IRS-compliant and can offer you all of the benefits highlighted above, it is essential that you obtain expert U.S. tax advice before you purchase an offshore insurance policy.

Some Things to Consider before You Buy

Before you buy a life insurance policy, consider your financial situation and the standard of living you want for your dependents or survivors. Ask yourself: Who will be responsible for your funeral costs and final medical bills? Would your family have to relocate? Will there be enough money for future expenses such as mortgage payments, and college? Reevaluate your life insurance policies every year or whenever you have a major life event, such as a marriage, a divorce, the birth or adoption of a child, or the purchase of a house or business.

What's the difference between an offshore variable annuity and an offshore life insurance policy? The chart below offers a brief comparison. As you can see, the two are very similar. The most significant differences come by way of taxes, policy minimums, and what your ultimate endgame is.

	Offshore Variable Annuity	Offshore Variable Life Insurance
Asset Protected?	Yes	Yes
Tax-differed Growth?	Yes	Yes
Income Tax on Payout to Heirs Upon Death	Yes	No
Medical Exam Required?	No	Yes
Estate Tax Avoidance?	No	Yes, with special structuring
Direct Investment Control	No	No
Minimum	As low as $100,000	$1 million +
Primary Objective?	To provide income upon retirement	To provide for your family upon your death

Tip
If you are not in good health, an offshore variable life insurance policy may not be an option, since you may not be insurable. The offshore variable annuity may be your only option.

OFFSHORE RETIREMENT PLANS

Your IRA, 401(k), or other retirement plan is more flexible than you ever thought possible. One way to gain investment flexibility and enhanced asset protection is to move your retirement plan offshore. It's a little-known approach, but it can spew out huge profits, demands less taxes, and plays a greater role in producing and managing your future income.

You're probably scratching your head right now. We don't blame you. We did that, too. We won't bore you with the details of the Internal Revenue Code that can give your retirement plan some very attractive advantages. Rather, we'll share with you the threats and challenges you potentially face as you approach retirement, and the solutions that are open to you.

The harsh truth is that there are two very real threats to your retirement account. The first is that you won't have nearly enough income to sustain yourself in your postcareer years. In fact, surveys repeatedly show that most people are *not* financially ready to retire especially with the latest market correction due to the current U.S. economic downturn. Second, your retirement assets are exposed to several risks. Over the past few years, all types of retirement plans have come under attack in the courts. Certain lawyers have made careers out of going after retirement plans just like yours. In fact, one very well-known attorney in the asset protection field said, "The successful attack on retirement plans is one of the fastest-growing areas of the legal profession."

Assets in employer-sponsored, tax-qualified retirement plans (e.g., pension, profit-sharing, and 401(k) plans) have generally been protected from the reach of creditors since the decision of the U.S. Supreme Court in *Patterson v. Shumate* (1992). However, IRAs are not covered. Therefore, the extent to which IRAs are protected has generally been a function of state law, which obviously varies from state to state. Although most states have statutes protecting IRAs to some degree, many of those statutes contain limitations, such as a fixed dollar amount or an amount determined to be necessary for the support of the individual debtor.

And it's not just lawyers you should be concerned with. You may think that you have plenty stashed away for a postcareer rainy day, but if your assets are denominated in U.S. dollars, then your retirement plan may already be in trouble. As you learned in Chapter 4, the long-term outlook for the U.S. dollar is pretty grim. If the U.S. dollar does plummet, then the value of your retirement plan will plummet right along with it. That only increases your chances of running out of retirement savings halfway through your retirement.

A Checklist to Ensure that You'll Have a Long, Well-Funded Retirement

First, assess where you stand in relation to your retirement goals. How much money have you saved? What will it be worth in the future? How much do you need to save and/or earn now to be properly funded for your retirement? Questions like these can put you on the right path toward your retirement.

Next, decide how much in today's dollars you will need to live on when you retire. The rule of thumb is between 60 and 90 percent of your preretirement income per year. Only you can judge if that's going to be enough. Statistics have shown that most people underestimate their spending—keep this in mind as you're calculating. Ensure that you are putting away as much as you can possibly afford. Find out if there is another retirement plan that would allow you to make a higher contribution than you are currently making. Every dollar counts.

Finally, make sure that your retirement assets are appropriately invested and in the best possible investment vehicles. If you are in a company plan and you can't control your own investments, talk to your plan administrator about modifying the plan to allow for self-direction and greater investment flexibility. If you are in a decision-making position, consider taking part of your plan offshore for greater investment flexibility. Or else diversify part of your portfolio into nontraditional investments that don't rely solely on a constantly rising stock market—think about things like precious metals, currencies, alternative investments, real estate, and principal-protected notes.

Fortunately for you, there are ways to maximize the potential benefits of your retirement plan to ensure that these threats don't affect the quality of your retirement years. If you seek positive investment returns, financial privacy, and a secure and prosperous retirement, it's time to move your retirement plan offshore.

The first step is to find the right custodian. As long as your plan is administered according to federal law, the investment options—and locations—are up to you. The Internal Revenue Code requires a U.S. custodian as part of a properly structured plan. The key to making this work is to use a custodian who understands the rules and is flexible enough to allow you to take advantage of these types of structures and investments. It is critical that you use an approved custodian who is in the United States at all times. Failure to do so can result in all of the plan assets being treated as a distribution—a most unwelcome event.

The Benefits of Offshore Investing for Your Retirement Plan

Investing offshore can triple the value of your retirement nest egg. You've learned that many of the world's best investments are available only beyond U.S. borders. With a few exceptions, U.S. law doesn't specifically address what investments you can place into a retirement plan. Instead, it lists various "prohibited transactions." Whatever is not prohibited is permissible. There are no specific rules prohibiting any offshore investment.

In other words, you can achieve all the advantages of offshore investments—higher returns, currency diversification, privacy, and asset protection—and not pay a penny in U.S. tax until you actually receive the profits. Indeed, if you make the investments through a Roth IRA, you'll *never* pay tax on the profits. Even estate taxes can be avoided with proper planning—and it's all perfectly legal.

Your U.S. broker probably won't tell you this, but it's absolutely legal to put offshore mutual funds, investment trusts, structured products, portfolio bonds, currencies, foreign annuities, and even real estate into your plan. Indeed, most investment restrictions are imposed not by U.S. law, but by domestic American custodians or retirement plan administrators. What's more, you'll pay no U.S. tax until you begin taking distributions from your pension plan.

Better yet, you can actually use your retirement plan to buy an exotic beachfront retirement home on a lush tropical island. Best of all, you can purchase this property with the tax-deferred dollars you've saved. You can even pay yourself a salary from your retirement account to manage the property. Your retirement plan can own any raw or improved land, condos, office buildings, single- or multifamily homes, and apartment buildings in any country, as long as the real estate is not for your current personal use. The only investments that a retirement plan can't make, domestically or offshore, are collectibles – like art, coins, cars, etc. – and some types of insurance. There are some restrictions on any investments you make with your retirement plan. These restrictions apply to real estate investments as well. One of the primary restrictions is that any investments that your retirement plan makes cannot be for your benefit today. They must be for the future benefit of you, your heirs, or both.

Move Your Nest Egg off the Radar Screen

Asset protection is another reason for placing your retirement plan offshore. Pension assets in the United States are at risk. Some retirement plans are protected, but many others are not. If a U.S. creditor obtains a judgment against your unprotected plan, forget all hopes of a comfortable retirement. Major corporations that are in financial trouble are abandoning their workers' plans and dumping billions of liabilities on the government and taxpayers.

Considerable asset protection advantages can be had by moving the assets of the IRA into an offshore structure. When your retirement plan purchases offshore investments, the assets are now held by a non-U.S. entity that is under no obligation to comply with the orders of a U.S. court. At the same time, your U.S. custodian remains responsible for complying with IRS reporting requirements. In many countries, it is against the law for an asset holder to comply with a foreign court order!

Reasonable folks want a shield against any snooping by business partners, estranged family members, or identity thieves. Financial privacy can be the best protection against frivolous lawsuits. If you don't appear to have enough assets to justify the time and expense of a lawsuit, you won't be the target of one. Assets that you invest offshore are far more private. There must be a catch, you're thinking, and you're right. There are a few eminently reasonable ones:

- *You must have a self-directed IRA, 401(k), or pension plan, or be able to convert your current retirement plan into a self-directed plan.* If you don't have one, it may be possible to "cash out" of your current plan and reinvest the money in a self-directed plan. There is no U.S. tax liability if the funds are reinvested in a tax-compliant retirement plan within 60 days.

- *No self-dealing is permitted.* For instance, you can't lend yourself money from an IRA and then use it to invest in your own business. However, there are numerous exceptions to the self-dealing rule.

- *You can't benefit from the investments in your plan until you actually retire.* For instance, if you buy an apartment in Vienna, you and your family (including anyone of direct "linear descent," and also your spouse, children, grandchildren, and so on) can't live in it until you receive it as a distribution from the plan. However, your siblings and friends can live in it legally—and are free to welcome you as a guest. There's an important exception to this limitation: you can make a temporary distribution of the apartment for up to 60 days, during which time you can live in it without any U.S. tax consequences. You can do this once a year, as long as you convey the apartment back to the retirement plan within 60 days of the distribution, in which case it's treated as a nontaxable event.

• *You won't be able to credit any foreign taxes you pay against your U.S. tax liability. This income is tax-exempt in the United States.* The countries you invest in will all have their own tax laws, and your retirement plan income is tax-deferred only in the United States. However, with foresight, you can often mitigate or even eliminate these taxes.

• *Distributions from a U.S. retirement plan don't benefit from the 15 percent tax rate for dividends and capital gains.* Instead, when you cash out, you'll pay tax on the income at your marginal tax rate, which may be substantially higher than 15 percent. However, it's often possible to plan distributions so that they take place in those years when your income from other sources is minimal. And of course, if you're taking distributions from a Roth IRA, there's no income tax to worry about at all.

The fees associated with moving your retirement plan offshore vary depending on your investments. For instance, if you buy securities through a foreign bank, you'll pay approximately 1 percent of the value of the account annually, plus loads (front-end or back-end), commissions, and service fees. If you purchase a foreign annuity, fees are around 1 to 1.25 percent annually, plus loads, commissions, and service fees. If you purchase an interest in a foreign business, you'll generally do so through an international business company (IBC). The fee to establish an IBC is typically $2,500 to $5,000, with annual fees and compliance costs of $1,500 to $2,000. Finally, there will be ongoing fees to ensure compliance with IRS rules and regulations. For most plans, these fees will be minimal.

A Final Word on These Offshore Solutions

We call offshore annuities, insurance policies, and retirement plans one-stop solutions for a reason. With any one of these little-known offshore solutions, you can secure an entire list of advantages, including

1. The last ways you can actually defer taxes.

2. The offshore investments that your U.S. Certified Financial Planner won't tell you about.

3. Real asset protection that you won't find in the United States.

4. A worry-free future with a well-funded retirement or hassle-free estate plan.

5. Financial privacy that could save you from costly lawsuits.

But please remember, when you're pursuing any of these solutions, you need to speak with qualified domestic and offshore professionals to ensure that you fulfill all your reporting and tax requirements.

CHAPTER

6

TAXES AND REPORTING: TAX SAVINGS, REPORTING RULES, AND USING TAX TREATIES

The late, distinguished Judge Learned Hand of the U.S. Court of Appeals in New York offered these timeless remarks: "There is nothing sinister in arranging one's affairs so as to keep taxes as low as possible . . . nobody owes any public duty to pay more than the law demands. Taxes are enforced exactions, not voluntary contributions."[1] In this chapter, you'll learn how to stay out of tax trouble by learning about avoidance, reporting rules, and how to use tax treaties to your advantage.

Far too many people get bad tax advice when they go offshore. There is so much information out there telling people that if they use offshore bank accounts, trusts or any other offshore structure,

---

[1] IRS Commissioner v. Newman, 159 F2d 848, 851 (2nd Cir 1947).

they do not need to pay U.S. taxes because the money is outside the United States. That's absolutely wrong. If that were true, everyone would put their money offshore. More than one person who has swallowed those lies sits in a federal jail convicted of tax evasion. The crooks who sold them the bad tax advice are also sitting in jail. As long as you know the rules and abide by them, you won't get into tax trouble. This is precisely why this chapter is vital to you and your future.

An Offshore First Truth

Americans who look for investment diversification or asset protection offshore usually don't receive much in the way of tax relief despite all the wild claims made by charlatans who promise that they can tell you how to avoid paying U.S. taxes! Take our word for it: U.S. taxes are tied to citizenship, and nothing can override that unless you choose to expatriate—which is tantamount to giving up your U.S. citizenship, passport, and residence. Even then, if the government feels you are expatriating to avoid taxes, you might still be required to pay taxes after expatriating. More on that in Chapter 8.

As we've shown you in previous chapters, investing offshore can

- *Defer taxes in some cases* (using annuities, life insurance policies, or retirement plans, as discussed in Chapter 5).

- *Exempt you from local offshore taxes.* That means that you won't pay tax in the local jurisdiction. For example, if you had a Panamanian business that didn't do business in Panama, it wouldn't be subject to Panamanian tax.

Living offshore can

- *Cut operating and living costs* for U.S. citizens living outside the United States.

- Permit U.S. citizens to *earn up to $85,700 annually free of U.S. tax obligations* ($171,400 for a married couple, both living offshore). To qualify, you must spend at least 11 months a year living outside the United States or be a "tax resident" in a country other than the United States.

U.S. citizens and U.S. resident aliens (green card holders) must pay annual income taxes (IRS Form 1040) on almost all the income they earn—no matter where in the world that income is earned, where they live, or where it is paid. That worldwide income must be reported to the IRS. Hiding cash, failing to file required reports, or failing to pay income taxes can result in fines, penalties, interest owed, and even prison, if you are convicted.

Neither investing nor living offshore can end or substantially diminish an American's income tax obligations. Eliminating taxes shouldn't be your primary motivation for going offshore. As we've mentioned several times throughout this book, the offshore world offers

- More investment opportunities
- Higher returns
- Currency diversification

- Safety and security

- Much stronger asset protection

- Real financial privacy

Before we get to the detailed tax info, let's start from the top. When you are trying to assess your personal tax situation, you must know the difference between what constitutes *tax avoidance*, which is legal, and what crosses the line into *tax evasion*, which is illegal.

But what is the letter of the law when it comes to taxes? Well, that's often more of a gray area than most of us like. Fortunately for us, there are qualified people who spend their entire professional careers deciphering the tax code. So what the heck do the 10,000+ pages of the U.S. Tax Code require you to pay Uncle Sam? We'll explain.

Tax Reduction: What's Legal and What Isn't?

Tax lawyers and accountants stress the distinction between two methods of tax reduction: *avoidance* and *evasion*. It's important to understand these distinctions and to realize their limits.

It looks simple, but there's a world of difference. *Tax avoidance* is using whatever *legal* means are available to minimize a tax burden; *tax evasion* is the use of *illegal* means toward that same end. It is legal when your accountant classifies your proven business or professional costs as "business expenses" on IRS Form 1040 Schedule C for the purpose of reducing your taxable net income. If the IRS disputes the deductions, you usually won't be indicted for a criminal offense. The worst that can happen is that you'll be asked to pay additional taxes and fees, even if you feel that's unfair. In the end, all you've done is engage in honest tax avoidance.

But on the proverbial other hand, if you willfully fail to report all, or even part, of your income on a tax return or fail to file the proper forms and reports, it's considered tax evasion. Good lawyers and accountants will work hard to help a client avoid taxes legally, using every possible accounting and legal loophole available. However, be warned: they want nothing to do with tax evasion schemes. They don't want to be accomplices in a crime that could destroy them professionally and send them to prison. And neither do you. You have an absolute right to discuss tax-planning possibilities that may seem legally dubious with your tax lawyer or accountant. This must be accompanied by a clear understanding among all parties that in no way do such talks suggest criminal intent. Knowing the difference between avoidance and evasion will promote such understanding. That's the principal key in all tax matters, foreign and domestic.

Remember the golden rule of offshore tax reduction: it's about legal avoidance and never about evasion. Uncle Sam will find you if you cross the line, and you don't want that. With good professional advice, proper planning, and accurate and honest reporting, the net profits offshore can be considerable—not to mention that better asset protection and greater privacy are certainly worth the extra work.

Take your time so that you, like thousands before you, will come out way ahead. Here are some ways you can benefit . . . .

You Can Earn $85,700 a Year—Free of U.S. Income Tax

If you work offshore, there's a whopping tax savings. If you qualify, you can earn $85,700 a year free of U.S. income taxes.

This is called the *foreign earned income exclusion* (FEIE). It allows any U.S. citizen who lives and works outside the United States to exclude up to $85,700 of income you earned while working abroad from your taxable gross income.

With a working spouse, you can get $171,400 annually.

$85,700 a Year Tax Free

To qualify for these benefits you must

- Establish a "tax home" in a foreign country.

- Pass either the "foreign-residence test" or the "physical-presence test."

- Actually have earned income for work.

- Be in the United States for no more than one month per year.

- File a U.S. income tax return for each year you live abroad.

This is not a tax deduction, credit, or deferral. It is an outright exclusion of the earnings from taxable gross income. There are no taxes due on this amount earned offshore. How valuable this tax break is for you depends on your *tax home*, the location where you and your regular, principal place of business resides. If you work overseas *and maintain a U.S. residence*, your tax home is not outside the United States. To qualify for the foreign earned income exclusion, *you must establish both your principal place of business or employment* AND *your residence outside the United States.*

To qualify for this foreign earned income exclusion, you must pass one of two tests established in the U.S. Tax Code:

- *Bona fide residence test.* If you have established legal residency in another country for an uninterrupted period of at least one year, you qualify under this test.

- *Physical presence test.* You qualify under this test if you are physically present in a foreign country or countries for at least 330 full days during any period of 12 consecutive months.

Things to consider when choosing a haven for tax purposes include the following:

- Does the country impose taxes on foreign investors? It's most advantageous for you to find a low-tax or zero-tax country.

- Are tax treaties or tax information exchange agreements with the United States in effect? Ensuring that there is means that you won't be taxed twice. If you pay taxes in the country you reside in, for example, Ireland, the U.S. will credit the taxes you paid to Ireland, on your U.S. tax return.

With these basics in mind, let's look at the details of the offshore tax situation. Ensure that you understand what taxes you owe as well as the strategies for handling them.

Reporting Is Required, Not Optional

So you've moved some (or a lot) of your cash and assets offshore. Do you have to tell the U.S. government that you have opened an offshore account or engaged in other offshore financial activity? If so, how do you report that?

The answer is yes, you must report it. You will most likely have more than enough cash in your offshore accounts to make them reportable to the IRS. U.S. citizens and permanent residents must report signatory or "other" authority (i.e., financial interest) over all foreign accounts that in aggregate exceed $10,000. There are two separate reporting obligations:

- You must acknowledge foreign accounts each year on Schedule B of your federal income tax return (due April 15 of each year).

- You also must file Form TD F90-22.1 (the foreign bank account reporting or FBAR form) with the U.S. Treasury Department (due June 30 of each year) for any reportable foreign accounts you had during the previous year.

There are three criteria for what constitutes a foreign account:

1. Any savings, demand, checking deposit, deposit, time deposit, or any other account with a financial institution

or other person engaged in the business of a financial institution

2. Any bank, security, securities derivatives, or other financial instruments account

3. Any accounts in which assets are held in a commingled fund and in which the account owner holds an equity interest in the fund

Additional reporting requirements apply to trusts and other international structures.

What Constitutes a Financial Interest?

- Joint accounts or partial interests in an account

- Agent, nominee, attorney, or in some other capacity holder of legal title on behalf of the U.S. person

- A corporation in which the U.S. person owns an interest in more than 50 percent of the total value of the shares of stock

- A partnership in which the U.S. person owns an interest in more than 50 percent of the profits

- A trust in which the U.S. person either has a present beneficial interest in more than 50 percent of the assets or from which such person receives more than 50 percent of the current income

- Signature or other authority over an account

The $10,000 account limit includes the total value of

- Cash

- Certificates of deposit (CDs)

- Any negotiable securities held personally in your name in any offshore bank accounts you control

It *does not include* foreign investments such as real estate or shares of stock held separately from the bank account itself. That would be the case if your bank purchased shares in the bank's name and held them on your behalf in a custodial account.

The Fine Print

Be careful of hair-splitting distinctions under the IRS foreign-account reporting rules. If you physically place your foreign bond or stock certificate in a safe-deposit box abroad, that doesn't necessarily mean that the value of those certificates counts toward a reportable offshore securities account. Check with a U.S. tax attorney to be sure.

What about Mutual Funds?

You must also report investments in most *foreign mutual funds* on IRS Form 8621. This is true whether you purchase the investments directly or through your foreign bank account. Since most offshore funds prohibit direct investments by U.S. persons, it is usually necessary to purchase the funds through a foreign account or, preferably, an offshore structure (like an annuity or retirement plan; see

Chapter 5). Keep in mind that any interest in a foreign mutual fund constitutes a foreign securities account and therefore counts toward the $10,000 limit for U.S. account reporting purposes.

Note that a mere *book entry* in a foreign corporation's records is considered a reportable other financial account if the corporation transmits or disburses funds or otherwise "functions as a bank" on behalf of the securities owner. It's a very close distinction, but one that you must be aware of.

Unfortunately, the IRS applies a very unfavorable tax regime to most foreign mutual funds unless you hold them in one of the tax-deferred vehicles such as a variable annuity or in your retirement plan. You shouldn't purchase foreign mutual funds without first obtaining expert tax advice. For offshore funds held for many years, the tax due can easily exceed the total gain, although the law provides that the tax and interest charge shall not exceed the total gain.

Nonreportable Offshore Investments

The good news is that not all offshore structures and investments are reportable. Here's a short list of what you currently are not required to report to U.S. tax authorities:

1. *Securities purchased directly from an offshore bank.* A securities account is a reportable account. But if you only purchase securities from an offshore bank, over the counter, without opening an account, and keep the certificates in your safe-deposit box, the reporting requirement doesn't apply.

2. *Real estate.* Direct ownership of real property in a foreign country isn't a foreign account. However, you are required to report income from your real estate holdings—wherever they are located.

3. *Valuables or documents.* Valuables (for example, colored diamonds or coins) or documents purchased outside of the United States and placed in an offshore vault don't constitute a foreign account.

4. *Warehouse receipts and similar instruments.* Certificates that represent ownership of precious metals or other commodities stored outside the United States are not reportable.

5. *Insurance or annuity contracts.* There is no mention of "insurance companies" in Treasury regulations pertaining to the foreign-account reporting requirements. However, a contract that contains securities (e.g., a variable annuity) may be reportable as a foreign securities account. Consult with a U.S. tax attorney to evaluate your particular tax situation.

If you have any questions about these rules, consult with a qualified professional, such as an international tax lawyer or accountant, to find out whether or not you need to file these forms. Do not rely on the staff of an offshore bank to guide you on U.S. forms or reporting requirements. You can't expect offshore banking professionals to provide expert advice on your particular home country's specific laws and regulations. Like most things in life, it's up to you.

Offshore Reporting to the U.S. Government

The following accounts/assets must be reported:

1. Bank, securities, or other financial accounts
   a. Check box "yes" on 1040B.
   b. File Form TD F90-22.1 annually if the amount is $10,000 or more.

2. This $10,000 or more includes
   a. Cash
   b. Certificates of deposits
   c. Negotiable securities in your name
   d. Mutual funds

There is no need to report the following list of accounts or assets. These refer to offshore investments that appear to be outside IRS reporting rules when they are purchased without opening a "bank, securities, or other financial account" or using such an account to maintain their custody. We say "appear" because you never know when the IRS will change the rules—a darn good reason to consult with experienced international tax experts. They are

• Offshore real estate.

• Offshore term life insurance policies or fixed annuities. (Most variable annuities and life insurance plans that hold securities are reportable.)

• Foreign securities purchased directly from a corporate seller.

• Shares held in a safe-deposit box.

GETTING PROFESSIONAL HELP

To comply with all but the most basic U.S. offshore reporting requirements, you'll need professional help, just as you may with your domestic U.S. tax returns. Generally it isn't necessary to obtain professional assistance to report a foreign bank account. However, you will definitely need help when you purchase offshore funds and any of the offshore structures we describe in these pages: trusts, offshore corporations, mutual funds, partnerships, and so on.

Few American tax attorneys or accountants specialize in offshore taxes or related matters. The majority of them will warn you against going offshore, not only because they don't understand this area, but also because they don't want to lose your business to offshore professionals.

You should explain to your local tax- or estate-planning attorney or accountant that you need him to work hand in hand with the offshore banks or other institutions you have chosen. By working together with these entities, he can do a better-quality job and perform a timely service. Most offshore professionals prefer to work with each client's local tax preparer to minimize the cost of the required work. Gathering, organizing, and analyzing the required information can probably be done by your local tax accountant. Examples include data on currency conversions, cost of assets, and analysis and compilation of basic foreign investment or bank account information from statements.

The following is a sampling of the kind of information required for most annual reporting:

- A brief description of your foreign investments, trusts, corporations, partnerships, or other entities, including the location and an explanation of who owns what.

- An explanation of your objectives in your offshore activities, the type of help you need, and special timelines other than the usual U.S. tax return filing deadlines.

- A copy of your most recent available personal tax return and any business- or trust-related tax returns or forms.

You should review and update this information periodically, keeping in mind the traditional U.S. income tax filing deadline of April 15, although many people seek an extension. Other foreign reporting forms are due annually on or before June 30.

USE TAX TREATIES — AVOID PAYING TAX TWICE

The next worse thing to paying taxes in your home country is paying taxes on the same income in two or more other countries. Bet you didn't think that was possible, did you?

Before you set up any offshore structure or account, study the tax arrangements before you leap. Careless arrangements can cost you unnecessary taxes that eat up the valuable offshore profits you earn. Strategies involving tax treaties aren't solely for offshore business activities, although this is their principal use. Depending on your business or the type of investment you make and the tax treaty that applies, your taxes may be much lower or, in rare cases, avoided completely.

Bilateral (two-country) tax treaties avoid double taxation imposed by two different nations that may have tax claims on you. Called "double tax treaties," they divvy up the taxing rights to different sources of income between the two countries. Generally, the country in which the income is earned (the source country) has priority taxing rights. The other country (the residence country) agrees not to tax that income, usually by giving credit for foreign taxes paid against domestic taxes that would otherwise be owed. Those are the basics, but the variations within each treaty can be huge.

Save Taxes with Double Tax Treaties

An American we know who earns income in Ireland pays the Irish tax rate of 28 to 40 percent, and then files with the IRS showing the amount of tax paid to Ireland. The IRS then gives him credit for the Irish taxes that he paid against any U.S. taxes that he might otherwise have owed. Result: no double taxation.

Dozens of U.S. tax treaties are in effect and are constantly renegotiated. Most of these treaties are with major industrial, commercial, and banking nations. Many other countries, particularly in Europe, have even larger tax treaty networks, notably the United Kingdom and the Netherlands.

We won't discuss each U.S. tax treaty here; the details of their application can be exceedingly complex, and they change often. Stay up to date by obtaining professional advice on any relevant tax treaty before investing, doing business, or moving your residence offshore. You can always find recent U.S. treaties on the Internet at the IRS Web site, http://www.irs.gov/.

Other Offshore Reporting Requirements

Form 720 for premiums paid to foreign insurance companies, unless payment of excise tax is waived under a tax treaty. In that event you must file Form 8833.

Form 926 for transfers of property to a "controlled foreign corporation"

Form 1041 to report the income and expenses of an offshore grantor trust. If the trust earns U.S. source income, it must file Form 1040NR annually.

Form 5471 annually for a controlled foreign corporation

Form 8621 to report income from, or dispositions, or a foreign mutual fund

Form 8832 to elect to have a foreign entity disregarded for U.S. tax purposes

Form 8858 annually for a disregarded entity

Form 8865 annually for a controlled foreign partnership

QI: THE QUALIFIED INTERMEDIARY RULE

In 2001, the U.S. Internal Revenue Service forced foreign banks and financial institutions into the unwelcome role of IRS informants, a.k.a. "qualified intermediaries" (known in the financial trade as "QI").

The result was that the IRS imposed extraterritorial tax enforcement burdens on foreign nations and their banks. It did this by forcing the banks to meet IRS-established "anti-money-laundering" and "know-your-customer" standards in order to obtain and keep QI status. Those offshore banks that qualify receive IRS "approved status." Banks that fail to obtain QI status are effectively banned from doing business in U.S. financial markets.

This IRS stamp of QI approval can seriously compromise or even eliminate client confidentiality if the U.S. offshore investor—like you—is not aware of these rules. It also gives the IRS leverage over foreign nations when demanding exchange of tax and other financial information, unless those nations have strict financial privacy laws.

Unfortunately, even in countries with strict bank secrecy laws, QI agreements have forced banks to require "secrecy waivers" from their U.S. clients. Virtually all offshore banks now require such a waiver if U.S. securities are purchased in the account. Some offshore banks even require such a waiver before opening the account or purchasing foreign securities.

The basic QI rules require U.S. persons owning U.S.-based investments purchased through offshore banks to choose to do either of the following:

- Allow the bank to report U.S. holdings to the IRS.

- Have the bank's U.S. withholding agent withhold a 31 percent tax on all interest and dividends paid, which the bank then transfers to the IRS without identifying the taxpayer.

There may be a way for you to avoid this. As a U.S. investor, you should not *buy U.S.-based investments through an offshore bank or financial institution* if privacy is important to you. Use an offshore account only for offshore investments. Otherwise, the offshore bank must report your investments to the IRS or tax you, as described previously. If you want to purchase U.S. securities, use a U.S. brokerage firm. This makes the most logical sense, and it keeps your offshore privacy intact.

TAX PRIVACY?

Under current law, the IRS has an obligation to keep any taxpayer's personal information that it has on file private. That's the law, but the history of the agency is rife with violations of taxpayer privacy. The bottom line: always report what is required, but seek professional advice on just how much you must tell the IRS.

ABUSIVE TAX SHELTERS

About a year or so ago, the *Financial Times* and the *New York Times* reported on so-called abusive tax shelters sold by major American accounting and law firms. While these were mostly domestic U.S. tax shelters, similar plans have been offered for offshore trusts and other offshore arrangements. Proceed with caution when tax plans are proposed that defy common sense, particularly when they are offered by "promoters" who lack training and experience in international tax matters.

What's the moral of the story? There are ways in which you can save taxes offshore, but you need to do it right and be sure you know what you can do and cannot do. *We repeat: tax treaties change constantly*. So do American domestic tax laws. What's here today is gone tomorrow. Serious offshore businesspeople and investors must be alert to tax changes the way they remain alert to weather and stock market reports. It's that essential.

CHAPTER

PERSONAL PRIVACY: IT'S STILL IMPORTANT AND AVAILABLE OFFSHORE

Privacy is an inherent human right—a basic requirement for maintaining our personal existence with dignity and respect. Privacy is the means by which we create and maintain our personal autonomy and individuality. We define our public face by exercising power over what personal information we voluntarily make available to others. A nation that is truly free does not force people to justify the choices they make about what personal and financial information they share and what they do not.

There was a time in the United States of America, and in other major nations, for that matter, when personal and financial privacy was taken for granted. Your personal life and your business were your own and nobody else's. In those long-gone days, your banker was discreet and hence would never discuss your financial affairs with anyone—certainly not with government agents unless they had a legal court order. Alas, that type of privacy no longer exists in America, especially when it comes to financial privacy and banking confidentiality. We'll explain why in a moment.

In our opinion, the right to privacy is not about covering up crime or wrongdoing. Privacy is important because it carries with it positive benefits. For example, anonymity protects your identity when you attend a political rally, visit a public space, or go to a club or bar. That kind of anonymity gives you privacy safeguards, personal safety, and peace of mind. Privacy also allows confidentiality, avoiding assaults on your person, such as the fastest-growing crime in America: identity theft and fraud.

A VIEW ON PRIVACY

In *The Fountainhead*, Ayn Rand said, "Civilization is the progress toward a society of privacy. The savage's whole existence is public, ruled by the laws of his tribe. Civilization is the process of setting man free from men." This begs the question, given modern times, of whether privacy in America is dead.

This is a simple question, and it has only one answer: yes. American privacy is dead. It's gone—*kaput, nada*, vanished. Even prior to September 11, American privacy was on the decline. After the attacks, the U.S. government and police became able to secretly tap your phones or e-mails, put key loggers on your computer, and search your office, home, and records of every kind. They accomplished this by using the USA Patriot Act as their weapon. For a relatively inexpensive fee, private parties can buy Internet and other searches that list every fact about you, your family, your finances, and even your personal music, video rental, and other buying habits. It's all perfectly legal. There's very little you can do to stop it—*but there are steps you can take to protect yourself.*

In an age of interconnected databases, electronic commerce, and instant worldwide communication, no area of financial activity offers more privacy and security pitfalls than personal and commercial banking. Once considered discreet and honorable, banks and other financial institutions are now required to reveal anything and everything about you to the government. Today your U.S. banker is obliged to report any "suspicious activities" to the federal money police daily.

When you cash a check or make a deposit of $10,000 or more in your U.S. bank account, that fact is electronically sent to the U.S. Treasury's Financial Crimes Enforcement Network (FinCEN).

FinCEN provides these data to more than 165 federal and local American law enforcement agencies, from the FBI and the Secret Service right down to your local sheriff and police chief. Even law enforcement agencies of foreign countries have access to these data under certain circumstances. The agency does this under a system that Congress and bureaucrats developed over the last 30 years, without any meaningful oversight from the courts.

FinCEN officials say that protecting the privacy of the information they receive from financial institutions is one of their top priorities. But we should ask how the agency does this? FinCEN shares its data on millions of U.S. citizens with intelligence agencies such as the NSA or CIA; they are generally prohibited from domestic surveillance, but the extent to which this prohibition is maintained is difficult to determine. The reason is that FinCEN has exempted itself from the Freedom of Information Act, Privacy Act, and other legislation that would otherwise permit disclosure of information to persons whose records are in its databases.

By setting up your financial affairs offshore, you can reestablish a much higher degree of personal and financial privacy. Smart, reasonable people understand the need for protection from the prying eyes of business associates, estranged family members, and identity thieves surfing the Internet. Your financial privacy can be the best protection against frivolous lawsuits that end with big judgments. If you look as if you don't have enough cash and assets to justify the time and expense of an attack by a contingency fee lawyer, you're not going to be a ripe target in his eyes.

Put Your Assets Where Privacy Really Lives

Good sense and self-preservation dictate that you reorder your wealth and assets so that a reasonable portion of them is located in an offshore nation where true financial privacy is guaranteed by law. To do this, you could use an offshore bank account, and even an offshore variable annuity or asset protection trust. You may also think about establishing your business or profession in an offshore tax haven. You even might want to consider moving to such a blessed country. There still are such places. (In Chapter 8, we tell you where these places are and how to get there.)

Until then, you're at the mercy of government and private snoops. You stand naked before the world. Feel that chill yet? You will.

The Offshore Privacy Vault

Many foreign nations not only preserve financial privacy, but do so as a matter of law. Anyone who violates that privacy is punished with fines and jail terms. In most of these privacy havens, only a court order can pry open your financial records. There are procedures that require that an individual be given notice of such inquiries and a chance to be heard in an official proceeding. In many offshore jurisdictions, a U.S. civil judgment will not be honored unless and until an entirely new trial is conducted under local law.

For example, since 1934, Switzerland has had a law that makes revealing financial information a crime. In Austria, strong privacy guarantees are part of the country's constitution and can be repealed only by national referendum. Similar privacy protections are written into the laws of tax havens such as Panama, Nevis, Andorra, and Monaco.

Therefore, it shouldn't take a lot of smarts to realize that it makes good sense for you to reorder your wealth and assets so that a reasonable portion of them is located in a jurisdiction where privacy is guaranteed by law. Until you do, you and your money are at the mercy of both government and private snoops. How can you reestablish real personal and financial privacy? The easy answer: move offshore with your cash and assets. As soon as you do, your privacy picture changes drastically. Let's explore this idea further.

Offshore Privacy for You and Me

For the average offshore investor or person who is financially active offshore, there is little to fear from the anticrime laws back home that have compromised our privacy. As long as you follow the financial reporting laws and tax obligations of both your home nation and the offshore nations where you do business, you'll be in the clear. If in doubt, seek professional advice. That will help ensure that you get it right.

One major point to remember: the financial privacy and bank secrecy laws of many nations are much stronger than those of the United States. For you, this represents a definite advantage—and an added shield for your financial activities and your assets.

Loose Lips

A leading European banker whom we know travels frequently. He admitted that whenever he's seated next to an American on a flight, it's only a matter of time before he knows the American's hometown, family history, profession, love life, and net worth. His advice: "Keep your mouth shut. Your business should be yours and nobody else's!"

Protect Your Wealth with These Simple Steps

You already know that it is in your best interest to conduct your financial affairs with the utmost privacy, caution, and discretion. Here are the legal and practical steps you can take to guard against being victimized by government and private snoops targeting you and your money.

To protect your privacy and wealth, consider these steps:

1. *Investigate, and visit, offshore banks* in jurisdictions that offer strong asset protection and real privacy guaranteed by law. Switzerland, Liechtenstein, and Panama are good examples of such places. We'll cover these jurisdictions in Chapter 8.

2. *Establish one or more offshore bank accounts* in certified, privacy-oriented nations. The nations mentioned previously are good examples, as is Austria. When this is done correctly, your cash and investments will be much more secure from almost all U.S. or other home-country-based claims and investigations. Do check out any foreign bank you consider using, and ask to see its written privacy rules and policies. Ask for references. (Refer to Chapter 2.)

Very Important

Never sign a bank's suggested waiver of your privacy rights. If it asks for such a waiver, leave immediately and find another bank.

3. *Understand foreign "due diligence" requirements.* With the end of totally anonymous accounts offshore, offshore

banks, like most banks, now require prospective customers to prove their identity with a certified copy of their passport or other official documents. They may also ask for a copy of a utility bill to prove your actual residence. You might also be asked about the origin of the funds you deposit in the account. A letter from your home-country bank may also be required. Answer all questions on the account application in full. Your responses and the documentation you provide are covered by the bank's secrecy laws in the jurisdiction you've chosen, so they remain private.

4. *Don't open an account at a foreign branch of a U.S. bank, or at a foreign bank that has U.S. branches.* Either of these factors places the bank immediately under the jurisdiction of the U.S. courts, opening the floodgates to litigants who welcome additional opportunities to penetrate offshore banking secrecy. Sovereign Society Convenient Account banking partners do not have U.S. bank branches, only representative offices.

5. *Don't use offshore accounts to hold U.S. securities.* If you do, that opens up a major hole in your privacy protection under foreign laws. The USA Patriot Act gives U.S. authorities the right to demand the identity of individuals with interests in U.S. "correspondent accounts" that offshore banks maintain for their customers who have U.S. dollar investments. In some cases, the U.S. government has also been confiscating

such accounts under the notorious "civil forfeiture" statutes. Also, IRS qualified intermediary (QI) regulations enmesh correspondent accounts in a maze of red tape. (See Chapter 6.) U.S. depositors in foreign banks who purchase U.S. securities and refuse to identify themselves to the IRS under the QI regulations are subject to a 31 percent withholding tax—not just on income from the account, but on all "broker proceeds" when they sell.

6. *Use attorney-client privilege.* This privilege protects the privacy of consultations with or under the direction of an attorney. Substantial privacy is also possible if you conduct business and financial transactions through an attorney. However, in virtually all jurisdictions, attorneys are prohibited from offering advice that would result in or encourage the commission of a crime. Attorneys in some countries are also required to report "suspicious transactions" by their clients to their domestic police authorities.

7. *Consider your overall estate plan.* As part of your overall estate plan, consider creating your own offshore corporation or family foundation to conduct some of your business and make investments. You might set up an offshore asset protection trust to hold title to specific assets. Many offshore havens allow the creation of these entities with a bare minimum of public records or none at all, thus protecting your privacy.

8. *Document all financial transactions precisely so that you always have ready proof that your activities are legal.* And by all means, have a coordinated last will and testament drawn up and revised regularly that takes into account your other estate plans and directs what you want done with the rest.

9. *Don't try to cheat the tax man.* Some high-tax countries, like the United States, impose taxes on the worldwide income of their residents. Domestic tax authorities like the IRS generally don't have the authority to go on fishing expeditions offshore to find unreported offshore income, but the trend is clearly toward more disclosure. So-called government antiterrorism legal and investigative tools are already being used to augment tax collection. Always report the existence of the account to your domestic tax authorities and pay whatever taxes are due. Follow the law so that no red flag is raised that could damage the privacy advantages of the account that is shielding you from possible private litigants.

10. *Consult an experienced professional attorney and/or accountant who has offshore experience before you take final action.* Know the U.S. or offshore tax implications of your plans. You may need two experts: one at home and another abroad. Obtain a firm and reliable estimate in writing of the cost of your plans, both (a) the immediate implementation costs and (b) the operation costs for the first few years.

ADDITIONAL PRIVACY STRATEGIES FOR DEALING WITH FINANCIAL INSTITUTIONS

On top of the suggestions just listed, here are a few extra tips you can use to maximize your privacy when contacting your offshore bank or other financial institution via e-mail or regular mail:

- *Get a post office box or mail drop* in your own name or that of your corporate or other entity. Bank statements and business documents can be a goldmine of information if they are opened by the wrong person at your actual home address. Don't send or receive mail from your home mailbox. Unprotected mailboxes are a prime target of identity thieves, who find it easy to steal credit card numbers, bank account numbers, and social security numbers.

- *Use encryption software.* Sending e-mail is the equivalent of sending a postcard: just about anyone can read it during its transit to its intended recipient. Protect yourself by using a free program called Pretty Good Privacy (PGP), which you can download at http://www.pgpi.com. A paid version that includes technical support is available at http://www.pgp.com. PGP is an encryption program. It converts your e-mail messages into unreadable gibberish that only the intended recipient of your message can decode. PGP also lets you encrypt files on your hard drive, so that only you can access them.

- *Use a firewall.* A firewall is designed to prevent unauthorized access to and from a computer or network. All data entering or leaving the PC or network must pass through the firewall, which blocks data that you haven't authorized to pass through. One firewall that detects both incoming and outgoing data is ZoneAlarm (http://www.zonealarm.com).

- *Consider obtaining a safe-deposit box at your offshore bank.* Keep special tangibles and other unique papers and property in it.

CHAPTER

8

ESCAPE TO THE WORLD'S BEST OFFSHORE HAVENS

We're almost at the end of our journey. You've come a long way! So far, you've learned what "offshore" means and where it is, reviewed specific offshore strategies, studied offshore bank accounts, explored legal entities of several kinds, and delved into the intricacies of offshore insurance, annuities, and investing. With all of this knowledge under your belt, it's time to set sail for the real freedom of the offshore world by selecting the appropriate jurisdiction for your offshore activities.

This may sound like the easiest part of your offshore quest, but while considering all the different havens is fun, this is a very critical step. It's a good idea to review your offshore goals. Whether you want ironclad asset protection, double-digit investment returns, financial privacy and security, or all of the above, it's important to ensure that the jurisdiction you select can satisfy all those needs.

In order to help you judge the various tax, asset, and banking havens objectively, we have examined the local laws, political stability, economic climate, tax situation, and overall financial "clout" of dozens of different jurisdictions. Based on our assessment, there are four particular havens that outshine the rest.

Top Offshore Havens

Drumroll, please—there are four countries that we feel are great places for you to consider for creating your personalized offshore plan: Switzerland, Panama, Liechtenstein, and Hong Kong. Before we get into the nitty-gritty of each of these havens, let's look at the five major factors we examined for each country and rated on a scale of 1 to 10:

1. *Government/political stability.* How long has the current system of government been in place? Is the jurisdiction politically stable?

2. *Favorable laws and judicial system.* How long a tradition has the country had? Does its legal and judicial system have a reputation for fair play with regard to foreign investors?

3. *Available legal entities.* Does the jurisdiction have a sufficient variety of legal entities to satisfy the average person seeking estate planning or business solutions?

4. *Financial privacy/banking secrecy.* Does the jurisdiction have financial privacy and bank secrecy laws? How strictly are they applied? What exceptions exist?

5. *Taxes.* Does the haven impose taxes on foreign investors or residents? How easily can these taxes be avoided legally? Are there tax treaties or tax information exchange agreements in effect?

Based on these important criteria, here is how the top four havens scored.

Switzerland: The World's Best Money Haven

Switzerland today still stands as the world's best all-around off-shore banking and asset protection haven, despite the many compromises that the Swiss have been forced to make under international pressure in recent years.

The Confederation of Switzerland is a survivor, and a wealthy one at that. Despite being surrounded by belligerents in World Wars I and II, it remained neutral in both conflicts and emerged with its infrastructure intact. Today, more than one-third of the world's private wealth resides in Swiss banks and fiduciary companies.

Switzerland is famous for its banking secrecy, and it has resisted decades of pressure from the Organization for Economic Cooperation and Development (OECD), the Financial Action Task Force (FATF), and other haven bashers to dismantle it. Financial discretion and unsurpassed professionalism in private banking and estate planning are the main reasons why wealthy investors have trusted Swiss banks for more than 200 years.

Switzerland today cooperates fully with foreign criminal investigations. It's no longer possible to have a truly anonymous Swiss bank account, and the country now participates in the EU Savings Tax Directive. EU nationals banking in Switzerland now have taxes withheld from most interest-bearing investments.

While Switzerland isn't a residential tax haven, there's an exception: wealthy foreigners who reside in Switzerland can be taxed on a lump-sum basis, starting at around $40,000 annually.

What to Do in Switzerland

1. Establish your personal residence with an agreed-upon annual tax.
2. Open a bank or investment account, if the high minimums (on average $250,000 or more) aren't a problem for you.

Panama: Switzerland at a Discount Price

Among current offshore tax havens, Panama combines maximum financial privacy, a long history of judicial enforcement of asset protection–friendly laws, and a strong anti-money-laundering law with tax exemptions for foreigners. Thanks to its unique historic relationship with the United States, it also exercises a high degree of independence from outside pressures, especially those from Washington.

Panama is truly a low-cost haven with 80 years of asset protection laws. It's less than three hours by air from the United States. It offers haven seekers a solid financial infrastructure, zero taxes for non-Panamanian income, low living and administrative costs, and one of the world's most attractive programs for foreign retirees, including discounts on many goods and services.

Panama is no late arrival among havens. Its corporation law dates to 1929, and the country has long offered refuge for entrepreneurs seeking to escape hyperinflation and foreign-exchange controls in Central and South American countries. More recently, Panama enacted a law authorizing private foundations—used like trusts in civil law countries—and patterned it after the best model available: Liechtenstein.

Panama has good offshore professional services, with dozens of banks, trust companies, and attorneys to choose from. You will need an introduction from a local source to open an account.

A central part of the long tax haven tradition has been statutory guarantees of financial privacy and confidentiality. Violators can suffer civil and criminal penalties for unauthorized disclosure. There is no requirement to reveal beneficial trust or corporate ownership to Panama authorities, and there are no required audit reports or financial statements. Bearer shares are still permitted. Panama has no double-taxation agreements and no tax information exchange agreements (TIEAs) with other countries.

Although it has been pressured by Washington to sign a TIEA with the United States, Panama has politely ignored such demands. Since 1904, the U.S. dollar has been Panama's official currency.

What to Do in Panama

1. Retire here or establish a second home under the *pensionado* program.
2. Acquire immediate residence status under several programs leading to citizenship.
3. Create a trust, family foundation, or international business corporation.
4. Invest in real estate.

Liechtenstein: The World's Oldest Tax Haven

With asset protection laws dating from the 1920s, a host of excellent legal entities designed for wealth preservation, and strict bank secrecy guaranteed by law, this tiny principality has it all.

Some say that this is a haven for aristocrats, and that's partly true. Its laws designed to shield privacy and wealth in the Principality of Liechtenstein date back to 1926, making it perhaps the world's oldest offshore haven. The British, Belgian, and Luxembourg royal families, among many other familiar names, are said to appreciate the professionalism, discretion, and secrecy offered by Liechtenstein and its unique entities. No wonder they feel at home—Liechtenstein has been ruled by the same aristocratic family for more than 800 years!

Prodded by the phony war on selected money-laundering centers, Liechtenstein no longer offers anonymous bank accounts or entities. It also ratified a mutual legal assistance treaty (MLAT) with the United States. Still, it remains one of the world's best locations for private banking and estate planning. And despite recent attacks on this small nation's bank secrecy laws after an incident with German authorities in early 2008, the nation refuses to surrender its strict bank secrecy laws.

In early 2008, the German secret police paid a disgruntled employee of one of Liechtenstein's most trusted banks, more than US$7 million to hand over a stolen CD. Supposedly, the CD contained confidential lists of the bank's foreign clients which allegedly contained the names of German citizens with accounts at the bank—a complete violation of Liechtenstein's bank secrecy and criminal laws. Based on the subsequent statements of the German Chancellor and her ministers that authorized the bribe, the official policy became "any German who has a bank account in Liechtenstein is judged guilty of tax evasion" and proceeded to threaten Liechtenstein with isolation in Europe unless the Alpine tax haven eased its bank secrecy.

You'll pay for the privilege of doing business here; fees and commissions are among the highest in the world.

Liechtenstein imposes no taxes on most entities owned by foreigners. However, it has signed on to the European Savings Tax

Directive and, like Switzerland, withholds tax from many interest-bearing accounts owned by EU nationals. Its only tax treaty is with Austria.

Liechtenstein's secrecy statutes have historically been considered stronger than those of Switzerland. The 2000 amendments to the money-laundering laws weaken secrecy significantly, but Liechtenstein still boasts some of the strictest confidentiality statutes in the world. While banks must now keep records of clients' identities, such records may not be made public. Secrecy also extends to trustees, lawyers, accountants, and anyone connected to the banking industry. In response to the 2008 incident with German authorities, Liechtenstein officials may also now allow very limited cooperation on tax information with foreign governments in individual cases. All are subject to the disciplinary powers of Liechtenstein's Upper Court.

A court order is required to release an account holder's bank records. Creditors seeking bank records face a time-consuming and costly process. Liechtenstein is not obliged to honor a foreign court's request for information. Such requests might be approved if it can be shown that a clear violation of Liechtenstein law has occurred.

What to Do in Liechtenstein

1. Open a high-dollar bank or investment account.
2. Create a trust or family foundation.
3. Purchase a variable annuity or life insurance policy.

Hong Kong: Special Administrative Region of the People's Republic of China

Even though the Communist government in Beijing controls it, Hong Kong remains relatively free, a reflection of Beijing's need for Hong Kong to be its financial powerhouse. Hong Kong retains a strong set of common-law statutes governing banking and finance. If you're doing business in Asia, especially in China, this is the place to be.

Hong Kong is a gateway for investing or doing business in China, but that's just one of its attractions. It's also a bustling, low-tax international financial center in every respect. Its reliable legal system, based on English common law, makes it a suitable jurisdiction for offshore companies, trusts, and mutual and hedge funds. Taxes are low to nonexistent. You pay 15 to 20 percent tax on personal or business income earned in Hong Kong, but no tax on overseas income and no death taxes.

For wealthy investors, Hong Kong is also a residential haven. If you invest the equivalent of $833,000 in the local economy and pass a background check, you can obtain a renewable residence visa. The only thorn: don't expect to find a cheap apartment—property prices are among the highest in the world.

Skeptics argue that Hong Kong's status as a "special administrative territory" of China might mean that Beijing could eventually curtail its freewheeling ways. If anything, this status helps protect Hong Kong from attacks by do-gooders at the OECD, FATF, and United Nations. You can count on Hong Kong to continue on its prosperity trail.

What to Do in Hong Kong

1. Create a corporation for business or investments in China, or in Asia in general.
2. Open a bank account for area or worldwide activity.
3. Obtain citizenship by investment and make your home there.

OTHER HAVENS OF THE WORLD

The four leading offshore financial havens just discussed are the cream of the crop. There are several others, however, and while they don't measure up to the "Big Four" in every respect, each has its own distinct attractions and services. On the flip side: in our opinion, some of the havens covered here have some flaws. We will point those out. In the end, the decision is yours and yours alone. At least, you'll be well educated—and enlightened.

The Isle of Man

The Isle of Man is a self-governing dependent territory of the British Crown; as such, it is not part of the United Kingdom, although the two are closely tied. The Isle of Man has a large and sophisticated financial center with a reputation for meeting all international standards, and is flexible and nonbureaucratic. The Isle of Man's financial industry has some 19 life insurance companies, 25 insurance managers, more than 177 captive insurance companies, 53 licensed banks, 82 investment business license holders and 164 collective investment strategies (mutual funds). It imposes zero taxes on corporations.

The Isle of Man is highly recommended for life insurance and annuities.

The Channel Islands

The Channel Islands, located between England and France, are autonomous possessions of the British Crown. The islands have their own independent government, with its own legislative, legal, fiscal, and administrative system. Britain is responsible for their external affairs. Under the UK's accession treaty with the EU, Jersey and Guernsey are part of the single EU common market but are outside the EU fiscal area.

Jersey is a highly developed and long-established international finance center, and its political and economic stability has made it an attractive base for thousands of banks, fund management companies, and other financial professionals. The island has developed a sophisticated and comprehensive infrastructure of laws and rules to support its finance industry and has particularly strong banking, investment fund, and trusts sectors.

As an offshore jurisdiction, nearby *Guernsey* is widely recognized as a well-regulated financial center with a very well-developed advisory and financial infrastructure. Guernsey is the home of the offshore operations of many of the world's largest banks, investment companies, and insurance companies. Jersey remains by far the largest of the British Isles' offshore jurisdictions in terms of its offshore deposits and mutual funds.

The Channel Islands are recommended in general, but keep in mind that they are continually under pressure from the British government to compromise financial privacy.

Gibraltar

Gibraltar is located at the southern tip of the Iberian Peninsula and has a landmass of 5.83 square kilometers (much like the famous "Rock of Gibraltar"). It has been a British colonial possession since 1713, and it is also a territory of the EU with UK accession. Spain wants control of Gibraltar, but in 2003, Gibraltar residents voted overwhelmingly by referendum to remain a British colony and against a "shared sovereignty." Spain disapproves of UK plans to grant Gibraltar even greater autonomy.

The development of a financial sector in Gibraltar has been helped by its location, a low-tax regime, a stable government, status within the EU, no exchange controls, a British legal system, and the availability of a qualified labor force. The financial services offered include banking, insurance services, fund management and insurance companies, and a modest investment and securities industry. In recent years it has become a favorite base of operations for foreign expatriates from Russia in particular, as well as for high-net-worth individuals from around the globe.

Gibraltar is recommended in general, but keep in mind that it's caught between Spanish demands for control and goofy EU rules that may force it to end its status as a tax haven.

Austria

Austria is not a haven in the sense of having low taxes, but it is an offshore banking haven. That's because this nation has one of the strongest financial privacy laws in the world. Privacy laws are written into the constitution and can be changed only by a national referendum of all voters. For the very wealthy, Austria also offers low-tax residency, if you qualify.

Austria is highly recommended for private banking and residency.

Andorra

Andorra is high up in the Pyrenees, nestled between Spain and France. It is a tiny country with no taxes, no army, and no poverty. It is a residential tax haven for very wealthy foreigners who enjoy winter sports. It's difficult to become a citizen, but establishing residency is fairly easy. The country's standard of living is high, while the cost of living is low and the scenery delightful, making it attractive. It provides political and economic stability: there are no strikes and virtually no unemployment, and it boasts the lowest crime rate in Europe. Remote Andorra could be your haven—and refuge—from the modern world's problems.

Andorra is highly recommended if you want strict bank privacy and residency in a no-tax haven—especially if you enjoy winter sports most of the year.

The Principality of Monaco

Monaco is a tax haven for the very wealthy—and great wealth is what it takes to live here. It is home to many millionaires, and even some billionaires, from around the world, many of them retired and enjoying the good life. Since 1869, there have been no personal income taxes for resident foreigners. Also, there is no direct withholding or capital gains tax for foreigners. It is easy to obtain residency in Monaco, but it requires a high net worth (at least $1 million or more), and fees are between $10,000 and $20,000. The Principality of Monaco is recommended for residency, if you can afford to live there.

The Bahamas

During the twentieth century, these islands off the southeast coast of the United States blossomed into a major tax and asset protection haven, especially for nearby Americans. They offered tax exemption for foreigners and a series of well-crafted laws allowing international business corporations (IBCs), trusts, offshore banks, and insurance—all wrapped in maximum financial privacy protected by law.

Because so many Americans used the Bahamas as their favorite offshore haven, the chain of islands came under heavy pressure from the U.S. government and the IRS because of suspected tax evasion. There were also issues of drug smuggling and money laundering. Starting in 2000, the Bahamian government adopted a series of U.S.-demanded laws that largely disrupted and seriously diminished the islands' role as an offshore haven. These changes were topped off with a Tax Information Exchange Agreement (TIEA) with the United States (good-bye, financial privacy!). The Bahamas are a nice place to retire, to vacation, or to have a second home, but more secure banking, investment, tax, and asset havens can be found elsewhere.

The Bahamas is recommended for retirement or vacation. It is not recommended for offshore transactions of any type.

The Cayman Islands

For decades, the Cayman Islands, just south of Cuba, were the premier jurisdiction of choice for tax-free international banking and businesses that desired ironclad secrecy guaranteed by law. They obtained it.

A few years ago, the Cayman Islands were home to the fifth-largest collection of wealth, including billions of dollars of assets under management. But a series of highly publicized cases involving drug and other criminal money laundering, plus a major case in which a local bank was used for wholesale U.S. tax evasion, forced the Caymans to give up financial secrecy.

As a UK colony, the Caymans are under extreme pressure from London and Washington, and this has weakened their financial and banking secrecy laws. As a result, billions of dollars have fled to more privacy-oriented havens.

However, the Caymans are still a tax-free haven for offshore bank accounts, trusts, and IBCs, as well as hedge funds, mutual funds, insurance, and annuities. After the media exposure of this haven, however, its name has become a red flag for foreign tax collectors everywhere.

The Cayman Islands are still recommended in general, but not for anyone seeking financial privacy.

Bermuda

Bermuda is 750 miles southeast of New York City and 3,445 miles from London. The island (57,000 people, 21 square miles) has enjoyed a long history of being a tax and banking haven. This is a world-class financial outpost, not to mention being a very pleasant place to visit or live in any season.

This mid-Atlantic island is the world's leading place for captive insurance used by businesses and for reinsurance. Bermuda offers excellent asset protection trusts and IBCs. Its three respected banks have worldwide branches and investment services. (One of them was purchased by HSBC.) Bermuda imposes no corporate income, gift, capital gains, or sales taxes. The income tax is extremely low—approximately 11 percent on income earned from employment in Bermuda.

More than 8,000 international business corporations call this island home, drawn by its friendly, tax-neutral environment, established business integrity, and minimal regulation.

Bermuda is also home to more than 600 "collective investment schemes" (a popular British Commonwealth phrase for mutual funds, unit trusts, and limited partnerships). With a statutory structure for protection, Bermuda is also a center for offshore trust creation and management.

But Bermuda has greatly diminished its haven status by signing a TIEA with the United States, making evasion of foreign income tax a local crime, and curbing its former financial privacy laws. Also, because it is a UK colony, Bermuda takes orders from London.

Bermuda is recommended for IBCs and insurance; however, it doesn't offer financial privacy. Bear this in mind when considering it as a possible jurisdiction.

Nevis

Located 225 miles east of Puerto Rico and about 1,200 miles south of Miami, Nevis is not well known outside offshore circles, but it's one of the best full-service tax-free asset havens in the world. For over two decades, Nevis has had asset protection–friendly laws allowing trusts, IBCs, and limited liability companies (LLCs). Its courts have an enviable record of support for offshore business, and its government is a strong offshore supporter as well. Any entity you need can be set up in a matter of a few days at minimal cost. It is also one of only two nations offering immediate citizenship. Nevis has only a few banks, but you can always bank elsewhere.

Nevis is highly recommended for trusts, IBCs, and LLCs. Also, it's a good place to consider for citizenship.

Belize

Belize is the only English-speaking nation in Central America. For more than a decade, it has had a series of offshore laws allowing asset protection trusts, IBCs, and insurance, as well as maximum financial privacy. Its parliament, courts, and government are very pro-offshore, and they cultivate foreign business and investments. An unusual feature is a special tax-free retirement residency program for foreigners. The country has three main banks, but they all leave something to be desired when it comes to service. Having said all that, this is definitely a third world country.

Belize is recommended with caution. It doesn't offer solid financial privacy and dealing with a third world country is not everyone's cup of tea.

U.S. Virgin Islands

It's not generally known, but under a unique special federal income tax arrangement applying only to the U.S. Territory of the Virgin Islands, it is possible for U.S. nationals and others who make the islands their main residence to enjoy substantial personal and business tax benefits. These lower taxes make the islands an offshore tax haven option for very wealthy U.S. citizens, U.S. entrepreneurs, and foreign nationals seeking U.S. citizenship. But the requirements are strict. You must actually make your primary residence there and invest a substantial amount—such as providing employment for locals.

The U.S. Virgin Islands are recommended for residency, if you're wealthy, enjoy golf and spending many days at the beach.

Singapore

Singapore is an island city-state in Southeast Asia, situated on the southern tip of the Malay Peninsula, and in many ways is a rival to Hong Kong. Established as a British trading port in the early nineteenth century, Singapore became a center of British influence in Southeast Asia. Upon achieving its independence from Malaysia in 1965, it developed into a successful free-market economy with one of the highest per capita gross domestic products in the world. It has excellent infrastructure, including an airport and a seaport that are among the best in the world, an extensive road network and subway system, state-of-the-art telecommunications facilities, and reliable public utilities.

Singapore's development as an offshore financial center began in the late 1960s. Today, there is a large and diversified group of local and foreign financial institutions, numbering about 500, located in Singapore and offering a wide range of financial products and services. These include trade financing, foreign exchange, derivatives products, capital market activities, loan syndication, underwriting, mergers and acquisitions, asset management, securities trading, financial advisory services, and specialized insurance services. Financial services account for 12 percent of Singapore's GDP. Singapore regularly ranks among the top 10 most sophisticated financial markets in the world.

Singapore has also become a private banking haven, with many Swiss banks opening large offices here.

Singapore is highly recommended for private banking and for financial services, especially if Asia is your area of interest.

Cook Islands

Located way out in the South Pacific, almost smack in the middle of nowhere, are the Cook Islands. They are home to a very modern set of offshore financial laws that may be just what you need—ironclad asset trusts, IBCs, limited liability partnerships, and a very strict financial privacy law that prevents revealing your personal business to anyone, including foreign governments. The biggest drawback is that most of us don't like too much distance between us and our assets, and these islands are very far out.

The Cook Islands are recommended, but only if you can deal with a long-distance relationship.

A Word to the Wise: Be Careful Which You Choose

We are almost at the end of your offshore education. On top of everything that you've learned up until this point, there is one more critical nugget of knowledge: the offshore location you choose is just as important, as what you do decide to do there. Don't make that decision lightly. Also always keep in mind that you don't have to do everything in one jurisdiction. You can pick and choose what's best for you from each of the havens.

Here are a few examples:

Example A

We know of a Canadian Sovereign Society member who came to one of our conferences in Panama several years ago. He had intended to stay only for the few days of the conference, but he wound up staying several weeks, then moving his home and his entire business to Panama. He's been there almost five years now to qualify for Panamanian citizenship.

Why would a Canadian want to move his business to Panama? One major reason: the nature of his business allowed him to restructure it in Panama with local employees, and because most of his business is done outside Panama, he pays no corporate taxes in Panama. The best part is that he no longer has to pay the high corporate taxes that Canada imposes—21 percent.

In addition, as a Canadian who moved away and established residence in another country, he no longer has to pay most Canadian income taxes. He has managed to do away with most of the 40 percent Canadian federal and provincial income taxes.

There is one other point of interest. While this member banks in Panama for his local needs, he also has investment bank accounts in Austria, Switzerland, and other offshore havens noted for their financial privacy.

Example B

Another Sovereign Society member, based in the United States, has been very successful in an international business. While his business makes a lot of money, it has an inherent liability factor that could cause him serious problems.

As a precaution, he has segregated his business and personal financial interests, using corporate structures that separate him from personal liability should anything happen.

His personal wealth is sheltered in two offshore trusts, one in the Cook Islands and the other in Nevis. Should anything happen to him, his trusts will limit the personal estate taxes that would otherwise be owed to the U.S. government and the government of the midwestern state where he lives. The rest will go to his chosen heirs—mostly family members.

Example C

It's a matter of record that in recent years stock markets in so-called emerging markets have made far better profits for investors than have the U.S. stock exchanges.

Another member we know, a person of modest but substantial wealth, realized this trend. She wanted to invest and trade offshore herself, completely unfettered, without having to go through costly American stockbrokers and mutual funds.

She started with an offshore bank account in Denmark and used it as a trading platform for buying and selling selected shares. Before long, she graduated to profitable currency trading, using her Danish bank account as her key to the financial world.

Of course, she has to report to the United States the profits from her offshore activity and the existence of her offshore bank account.

CONCLUSION

THE LAST WORD

Well, now you know all about offshore. It may have occurred to you as you've progressed through this book that some of the places we discussed could turn out to be an interesting location for a second home, vacation destination, or even as a place to retire and enjoy life.

Your obvious choice would certainly be to locate in a tax-free or low-tax haven where you could enjoy the good life and save money. Consider whether you would like to do any of the following things.

LIVE IN A TAX HAVEN

Foreigners who move their residence to a tax haven not only save taxes, but can also live at a far lower cost in retirement than they can in the high-cost, high-tax United States. In fact, legions from the so-called baby-boom generation of Americans born after World War II are flocking to retirement in Panama, Mexico, Nicaragua, and other Central American and Caribbean nations.

Even though U.S. citizens are taxed on their worldwide income, there are many attractive places to live where taxes on business activities conducted away from America can be reduced or deferred. These places exempt foreigners from income and business taxes and from many other local taxes.

Numerous countries provide at least limited tax incentives to new residents because they want to create more jobs for locals, as well as to import more dollars. It's easy to qualify in such places if you're healthy and you have sufficient income and assets that you won't need a job in the local market. Some countries do grant work permits for certain occupations.

There are a few countries that offer low taxes and a high quality of life with a wide range of amenities, excellent medical facilities, easy residence requirements, and a warm climate, all within easy reach of American major cities.

Panama Stands Out

Panama offers one of the most attractive locations in the Americas. It has a special *pensionado* program that provides foreign retirees with tax-free living and discounts on many goods and services. Residents pay no tax on income earned outside Panama, even if that offshore income is brought into the country. You also have the option of acquiring residence as a financially independent person/retiree or investor.

Belize offers a similar special program consisting of zero taxes and other incentives for foreign retirees. For people of great wealth, both Austria and Switzerland have special immigration and tax arrangements for foreigners who wish to make their home or retire there.

For more information about offshore residency, contact The Sovereign Society by visiting us at www.sovereignsociety.com.

DUAL CITIZENSHIP

If you decide to take up residence in an offshore tax haven, you might also consider obtaining a second passport and dual citizenship. Under U.S. law, dual citizenship is legal, as it is under the laws of many nations. If you're considering expatriation (discussed later), a second citizenship is a must.

Acquiring a second nationality is a hedge against unknown events. It gives you the option of residing in another country that may offer tax advantages, although this is of little benefit to U.S. citizens.

You may be able to acquire a second nationality and passport based on ancestry (Ireland), marriage (some EU nations), or religious affiliation (Israel). If you don't qualify on these grounds, your options are limited to obtaining citizenship by living in a place for a period of time (anywhere from 2 to 12 years, depending on the nation) or obtaining citizenship by investment. "Citizenship by investment" is the granting of citizenship by a country in exchange for a financial contribution to that country, or for making an investment in a business, real estate, or other officially designated project within that country.

At present, St. Kitts and Nevis and Dominica, both Caribbean island nations, are the only countries that offer immediate legal citizenship by investment programs. In Austria, it is also possible, under certain conditions and on an individual case basis, to obtain citizenship without prior residence in return for a substantial investment. All these programs require applicants to pass a rigorous screening process.

- *St. Kitts and Nevis.* This passport has a good reputation and allows travel to most countries without a visa. It requires a real estate investment of at least US$350,000, plus application fees that total US$35,000 for a single applicant plus US$15,000 for each dependent, plus a "due diligence" fee of US$2,000 per adult applicant. Or you can contribute US$200,000 (for a single applicant) to the Sugar Industry Diversification Foundation.

- *Commonwealth of Dominica.* Two options are offered for citizenship by investment: a family option (requiring a payment of US$150,000) and a single option (requiring a payment of US$75,000). Application, agent, and registration fees are approximately US$17,000. You must also go to Dominica for an interview.

- *Austria.* Here you may qualify for citizenship if you make a substantial investment that creates jobs. There is no "program" as such, and few cases are approved each year. An equity investment of approximately US$1 million is normally required, along with application and legal fees of approximately US$250,000.

- *Switzerland.* Foreign people of wealth can negotiate both residence and an annual tax payment.

EXPATRIATION: THE ULTIMATE ESTATE PLAN

Expatriation means "to remove oneself from residence in one's native land." In a legal sense, it means that a person voluntarily ends his native or adopted citizenship. For Americans, expatriation has been called "the ultimate estate plan." It's a step-by-step process that can lead to your legal right to stop paying U.S. or other home-country income taxes—forever.

This process requires professional help, careful planning, movement of assets offshore, and the acquisition of a new, second nationality. When all that is done properly, you must leave your home country behind and become a "tax exile" with an established domicile in a low- or no-tax jurisdiction. For U.S. citizens, this unusual plan requires a final step toward tax freedom: *the formal cessation of citizenship in the United States of America.* A drastic plan? You bet!

Yes, there are many other suitable offshore strategies that can give you significant tax savings or deferrals, including offshore life insurance policies or annuities and offshore investments made through U.S.-based retirement plans. But for the U.S. citizen who wants a permanent and legal way to stop paying U.S. taxes, the only option is expatriation. Here's why expatriation is often of interest to wealthy Americans: a few years ago a *Forbes* magazine article gave the compelling arithmetic. "A very rich citizen of The Bahamas pays zero estate taxes whereas a rich American—

anyone with an estate worth US$3 million or more—could pay up to 55%." Even though U.S. estate taxes have decreased in recent years, expatriation allows you eventually to escape American income, capital gains, and other taxes.

Substantial tax savings are available for wealthy U.S. citizens who are prepared to give up their citizenship. While only a handful of very rich Americans have legally expatriated, these individuals include some prominent names.

In 1962, John Templeton, a respected international investor, businessman, and philanthropist, surrendered his U.S. citizenship to become a citizen of the Bahamas. This move saved him more than US$100 million when he sold the well-known international investment fund that still bears his name.

As we go to press, there is a bill that's been approved by Congress that will require future expatriates to pay a tax on *all* unrealized gains on their *worldwide estate*, including most offshore trusts. And the tax applies not only to former U.S. citizens, but also to long-term green card holders who have resided in the United States for at least 8 of the 15 years preceding expatriation. (Fortunately, long-term residents can "opt out" of the exit tax, as I'll explain in a moment.)

How are you supposed to pay the tax without selling your assets? That's your problem—not the IRS's—although the bill permits deferral in certain circumstances.

The Exit Tax Isn't Just for the Wealthy
It would be one thing if the exit tax affected only billionaires. But, with only a few exceptions for dual nationals and others with

strong ties to another country, the tax applies to any expatriate who:

1. Has an average annual net income tax liability for the five preceding years ending before the date of the loss of U.S. citizenship or residency termination that exceeds US$139,000, adjusted annually for inflation.

2. Has a net worth of US$2 million or more on such date.

3. Fails to certify under penalties of perjury that he has complied with all U.S. federal tax obligations for the preceding five years or fails to submit any proof of compliance that the IRS demands.

If you qualify under any of these criteria, you may be subject to the exit tax. The good news—if there is any—is that the first US$600,000 of gains is excluded. This exclusion doubles to US$1.2 million for a married couple filing jointly, both of whom expatriate. This exclusion will increase by a cost of living adjustment factor after 2008.

Gains will be calculated on a "mark-to-market" basis, i.e., the difference between the market value on the date of expatriation and the market value at acquisition. Expatriates who were not born in the United States may elect to value their property at its fair market value on the date they first became U.S. residents, rather than when they first acquired the property.

This phantom gain will presumably be taxed as ordinary income (at rates as high as 35 percent) or as capital gains (at either a 15 percent, 25 percent, or 28 percent rate), as provided under current law. When you actually sell the assets, no additional U.S. tax is due. However, your adopted country might tax the gain a second time, leading to double taxation on the same income.

Your Retirement Plan Takes a 51 Percent Hit

And now for the really bad news: once you expatriate, you'll pay up to a 51 percent tax on distributions from most retirement plans and most other forms of deferred compensation. If there's a silver lining, it's that the tax isn't due until you actually receive payments from the plan.

Plans covered by this provision include

- Qualified pension, profit-sharing, and stock bonus plans
- Qualified annuity plans
- Federal pension plans
- Simplified employee pension plans
- Simplified retirement accounts

The tax is imposed in two steps. The entity responsible for making the payment must withhold a 30 percent tax from any distributions to a "covered expatriate." That entity must also withhold a second 30 percent tax for payments to a "nonresident alien individual." Applying these two taxes sequentially results in a 51 percent net tax.

Similar rules (but with some added complexities) apply for distributions from nongrantor trusts, i.e., trusts for which an expatriate is not treated as the owner under the grantor trust rules.

Your individual retirement account is *not* eligible for this treatment. If you're a "covered expatriate," you must pay income tax on the entire value of the plan, as if you received it in a lump sum. (Fortunately, no early distribution tax applies if you're under age 59$^{1}/_{2}$.)

Strategies to Avoid the Exit Tax and More

If your net worth is only a little over US$2 million (US$4 million for a married couple expatriating at the same time), the most obvious way to avoid the exit tax is to spend enough money to get your net worth under these thresholds. Take a trip around the world. Blow some money in Las Vegas. Throw a really big party.

You can also contribute your excess funds to a qualified charity, or give away up to US$1 million over your lifetime to anyone else without triggering a gift tax liability.

If you've paid more than an average of US$139,000 in taxes annually for the previous five years, however, this strategy won't work. And if you don't have sufficient cash to pay the exit tax, your best option may be to elect to defer payment. You'll pay interest for the period the tax is deferred, and you may be required to post a bond with the Treasury Department.

Fortunately, you can make this election (which is irrevocable) on a property-by-property basis. For instance, it appears that you could pay the exit tax on all assets outside your IRA and defer it for the assets in the IRA.

If you weren't born in the United States, you have a couple of additional options.

- If you were born with citizenship in both the United States and another country, you may not be subject to the exit tax. To qualify for this exemption, when you expatriate, you must also be a citizen of another country (and taxed by another country), and not have been a U.S. resident for more than 10 years during the 15-year period prior to your expatriation.

- If you're a green card holder, you can opt out of the exit tax. To do so, you must become resident for tax purposes in a foreign country that has a tax treaty with the United States. You must also inform the IRS of your intention not to waive the benefits of the tax treaty applicable to that country.

The bottom line: with this exit tax, Congress has made the most significant change in the antiexpatriation rules since their inception in 1966. In doing so, it's sent wealthy U.S. citizens and long-term residents a clear message: if you want to exercise your right to leave, you'll pay dearly for the privilege.

Is expatriation for you? The decision to give up your U.S. citizenship is a serious one. It requires that you obtain a passport from another country, leave the United States permanently, and set up residence in a suitable jurisdiction. It's a step that you should take only after consulting with your family and professional advisors. But it's the only way in which U.S. citizens and long-term residents can legally eliminate their U.S. tax liability. And it's a tax avoidance option that Congress has now made much more difficult.

The 5 Key Steps to Expatriation

If you really want to expatriate, you must reorder your financial affairs long before you formally give up your U.S. citizenship. This is to remove most, if not all of your assets, from government control and taxation. Here are some of the steps:

1. Arrange your affairs so that most or all of your income is derived from non-U.S. sources.

2. Title your property ownership in such a way that any assets that remain in the United States are exempt from U.S. estate and gift taxes.

3. Move abroad and make your new home in a no-tax foreign nation so that you are no longer considered a U.S. resident.

4. Obtain another citizenship and the second passport that comes with it.

5. Finally, surrender your U.S. citizenship after changing your legal domicile to your new nation.

Here's what the process and the timetable look like:

- Decision to expatriate leading to consultation with expert advisors: one to two years prior to expatriation.

- Liquidation of U.S. assets: one to two years prior to expatriation.

- Selection of appropriate jurisdictions for alternative citizenship and residency: one to two years prior to expatriation.

- Move to selected residency haven leading to alternative citizenship: up to ten years.

- Surrender U.S. citizenship.

Where do you want to go?

One of the most important decisions you're going to make is your choice of a second nationality. Millions of Americans already hold a second nationality; millions more qualify almost instantly by reason of birth, ancestry, or marriage. For instance, in many countries, like Ireland, having a parent or grandparent born in that country will qualify children or grandchildren for immediate citizenship and passport after presenting the appropriate documentation.

Otherwise, you will need to qualify for a second citizenship through residency (2 to 12 years) in a country based on your economic status or investments you make there. Both Panama and Belize have formal tax-advantaged immediate residency plans for foreign nationals who wish to make their home there, but they do not lead to citizenship.

Or you may choose to purchase economic citizenship, which can be obtained in a matter of months, but only at significant cost. As mentioned earlier, the only two economic citizenship programs still offered are from the Commonwealth of Dominica and St. Kitts and Nevis.

This may seem like a pipedream, and admittedly it takes a sense of adventure and courage to make major changes in your life. But now that you know what treasures lie offshore, you may be able to find your own Treasure Island.

Now, It's All Up to You!

These are just a few examples of what can be done—and what you can do. The possibilities are limited only by your ability to use the knowledge you have gained from these pages.

Get going! Good luck and bon voyage!

GLOSSARY

Acceptance: Unconditional agreement by one party (the offeree) to the terms of an offer made by a second party (the offeror). This agreement results in a valid, binding contract.

Arbitrage: Buying securities in one nation, currency, or market and selling them simultaneously in another to take advantage of the price differential.

Attachment: The postjudicial civil procedure by which personal property is taken from its owner pursuant to a judgment or other court order.

Basis: The original cost of an asset, used to measure its increased value for tax purposes at the time of sale or disposition.

Bearer bonds: A negotiable stock certificate made out only to bearer, without designating the shareowner by name. Such shares are not registered with the issuing company, and dividends are claimed by clipping coupons attached to the shares and presenting them for payment.

Beneficiary: One who is designated to receive income from a trust or estate; a person named in an insurance policy to receive proceeds or benefits.

Bequest: A gift of personal property by will; also called a legacy.

Capital gain: The amount of profit earned from the sale or exchange of property, measured from the original cost basis.

Captive insurance company: A wholly owned subsidiary company established by a noninsurance parent company to spread insured risks among the parent and other associated companies.

Civil suit: A noncriminal legal action between parties relating to a dispute or injury, in which one party is seeking remedies for a violation of contractual or other personal rights.

Common law: The body of law developed in England through judicial decisions based on customs and precedent; it forms the basis of the present English, British Commonwealth, and U.S. legal systems. See also *equity*.

Community property: In certain states in the United States, property acquired during marriage that is jointly owned by both spouses, each with an undivided one-half interest.

Contract: A binding agreement between two or more parties; also, the written or oral evidence of an agreement.

Corporation: A business, professional, or other entity recognized in law as acting as a single and separate legal person, although composed of one or more natural persons, and endowed by law with various rights and duties, including the right of succession.

Corpus: The property owned by a fund, trust, or estate; also called the principal.

Creator: See *grantor.*

Creditor: One to whom a debtor owes money or other valuable consideration.

Currency: Official, government-issued paper and coins; hard currency describes a national currency that is sufficiently sound to be generally acceptable in international dealings.

Debtor: One who owes another (the creditor) money or other valuable consideration, especially one who has failed to make payments that are due.

Decedent: A term used in estate and probate law to describe a deceased person.

Declaration: A formal statement in writing of any kind, often signed and notarized, especially a document establishing a trust; also called an indenture or trust agreement.

Deed: A formal written document signed by the owner of real estate conveying title to that real estate to another party.

Domicile: A person's permanent legal home, as compared to a place that may be only a temporary residence. A person's domicile determines what law applies to that person for purposes of marriage, divorce, succession of the estate at death, and taxation.

Equity: A body of judicial rules developed under the common law that is used to enlarge and protect legal rights and enforce duties while seeking to avoid the unjust constraints and narrowness of statutory law; also, the unrealized value of a person's investment or ownership, such as a trust beneficiary's equitable interest; also, the risk-sharing part of a company's capital, referred to as ordinary shares.

Estate: Any of various kinds or types of ownership that a person may have in real or personal property; often used to describe all property of a deceased person, meaning the assets and liabilities remaining after death.

Estate tax: Taxes imposed at death by the U.S. and most state governments on the assets of a decedent, except on the first US$2 million in value (for 2008). The exempt amount by law will increase annually until it reaches US$3.5 million in 2009 at which point it will be repealed in 2010 unless Congress votes to uphold the existing exemptions.

Exchange controls: Government restrictions imposed on dealings in a national or foreign currency.

Executor: The person who manages the estate of a decedent; also called an executrix (if a female), personal representative, administrator, or administratrix (if a female).

Exemption: In tax law, a statutorily defined right to avoid the imposition of part or all of certain taxes; also, the statutory right granted to a debtor in bankruptcy to retain a portion of her real or personal property free from creditors' claims.

Expatriation: The transfer of one's legal residence and citizenship from one's home country to another country, often in anticipation of government financial restrictions or taxes.

Family partnership (also, family limited partnership): A legal business relationship created by agreement among two or more family members for a common purpose; often used as a means of transferring and/or equalizing income and assets among family members so as to limit individual personal liability and taxes. See also *partnership* and *limited partnership*.

Fiduciary: A person holding title to property in trust for the benefit of another, such as a trustee, guardian, or executor of an estate.

Gift tax: A U.S. tax imposed on any gift made by one person to another person that is in excess of US$10,000 annually.

Grantor: A person who conveys real property by deed; a person who creates a trust; also called a trust donor or settlor.

Grantor trust: As used in U.S. tax law, an offshore trust, the income of which is taxed by the IRS as the personal income of the grantor.

Gross estate: The total value for estate tax purposes of all of a decedent's assets, as compared to net estate, the amount remaining after all permitted exemptions, deductions, taxes, and debts owed.

Guardianship: A power conferred on a person, the guardian, usually by judicial decree, giving that person the right and duty to provide personal supervision, care, and control over another person who is unable to care for herself because of some physical or mental disability or because of minority age status.

Haven or haven nation: A country in which banking, tax, trust, and corporation laws are specially designed to attract foreign persons who wish to avoid taxes or protect assets.

Incorporation: The government registration and qualification process by which a corporation is formed under law.

Indemnity: An agreement by which one entity promises to protect another from any loss or damage; usually used to describe the role of the insurer in insurance law.

Indexes of ownership: Factors indicating a person's control over, and therefore ownership of, property, especially trust property, including the power of revocability.

Inheritance tax: A tax imposed by government on the amount a person receives from a decedent's estate, rather than on the estate itself.

Insurance: A contract or policy under which a corporation (the insurer) undertakes to indemnify or pay a person (the insured) for a specified potential future loss in return for the insured's payment of an established sum of money (the premium).

Interbank rate of exchange: The interest rate that banks charge each other in their dealings.

Interest: A right, title, or legal property share; also, a charge for borrowing money, usually a percentage of the total amount borrowed.

International business corporation (IBC): A term used to describe a variety of offshore corporate structures characterized by having all or most of their business activity outside the nation of incorporation and offering maximum privacy, flexibility, low or no taxes on operations, broad powers, and minimal filing and reporting requirements.

Irrevocable trust: A trust that, once established by the grantor, cannot be ended or terminated by the grantor.

Joint tenancy: A form of property co-ownership in which each party holds equal title with the right of survivorship; a tenancy by the entireties is a similar type of tenancy that is reserved to husband and wife in some American states.

Judgment: An official and authenticated decision of a court.

Jurisdiction: The statutory authority that a court exercises; also, the geographic area or subject matter over which a government or court has power.

Last will and testament: A written document in which a person directs the postmortem distribution of his property. In the United States, state law governs the specific requirements for a valid will.

Legal capacity: The competency or ability of parties to make a valid contract, including being of majority age (18 years old) and being of sound mind.

Life estate: The use and enjoyment of property granted by the owner to another during the owner's life or during the life of another, at the termination of which, title passes to another, known as the remainderman.

Life insurance trust: An irrevocable living trust that holds title to a policy on the grantor's life, the proceeds of which are not part of the grantor's estate.

Limited partnership: A partnership in which certain individuals, known as limited partners, have no management role, but receive periodic income and are personally liable for partnership debts only to the extent of their individual investment.

Money laundering: The process of concealing the criminal origins or uses of cash so that it appears that the funds involved come from legitimate sources; it is a crime in most major nations.

Mutual legal assistance treaty (MLAT): A bilateral treaty between nations governing cooperation in international investigations of alleged criminal conduct.

Numbered bank account: Any account in a financial institution that is identified not by the account holder's name, but by a number, limiting knowledge of the owner's identity to a few bank officials. While these accounts are often associated with Swiss banking, they are also available in some other asset haven nations.

Offshore asset protection trust (APT): An offshore trust that holds title to and protects the grantor's property from claims, judgments, and creditors, especially because it is located in a country other than the grantor's home country.

Power of attorney: A written instrument allowing one to act as agent on behalf of another; the scope of the agency power is indicated by the terms, known as general or limited powers.

Preservation trust: Any trust designed to limit a beneficiary's access to income and principal.

Primary residence: Especially in tax law, a home place, as compared to a vacation or second home. See *domicile*.

Probate: A series of judicial proceedings, usually in a special court, initially determining the validity of a last will and testament, then supervising the administration or execution of the terms of the will and the decedent's estate.

Protector: In offshore haven nations, an appointed person who has the duty of overseeing the activities of an offshore trust and its trustee.

Quitclaim deed: A deed transferring any interest that a grantor may have in real property without guarantees of title, if in fact any interest does exist.

Real estate investment trust (REIT): An investment fund in trust form that owns and operates real estate for shareholding investors who are the beneficiaries.

Remainder: In testamentary law, the balance of an estate after payment of legacies; in property law, an interest in land or a trust estate distributed at the termination of a life estate. A person with a right to such an estate is a remainderman.

Revocable trust: A living trust in which the grantor retains the power to revoke or terminate the trust during her lifetime, returning the assets to herself.

Right of survivorship: An attribute of a joint tenancy that automatically transfers ownership of the share of a deceased joint tenant to the surviving joint tenants without the necessity of probate.

Spendthrift trust: A restricted trust created to pay income to a beneficiary who is judged by the trust grantor to be too irresponsible to handle his own personal economic affairs.

Subchapter S corporation: Under U.S. tax law, a small business corporation that elects to have the undistributed taxable income of the corporation taxed as personal income of the shareholders, thus avoiding payment of corporate income tax.

Trust: A legal device allowing title to and possession of property to be held, used, and/or managed by one person, the trustee, for the benefit of others, the beneficiaries.

Unit trust: In the United Kingdom and in Commonwealth nations, the equivalent of the type of investment fund known in the United States as a mutual fund.

U.S. person: For U.S. tax purposes, any individual who is a U.S. citizen; a U.S. resident alien deemed to be a permanent resident; or a U.S.-domiciled corporation, partnership, estate, or trust.

INDEX

ABOUT THE AUTHORS

ERIKA NOLAN

With over 15 years of marketing, public relations, and international business experience, Erika Nolan is a seasoned executive. She spent four years in the health-care industry as a public relations and marketing executive for a US$3 billion, publicly traded company, acting as the company spokesperson and directing all its marketing strategies.

In 1998, she was recruited to be the Managing Director for The Sovereign Society (www.sovereignsociety.com), an offshore, asset protection and international finance organization. She has brought with her an extensive knowledge of marketing and operational expertise, which has led to a high record of success.

During her tenure with The Sovereign Society, she has created a highly respected global network of experts to best service the needs of the Society's members and to advise on best practices in the offshore world. She travels extensively throughout Europe, Asia, the Caribbean, and Central America and speaks at various seminars and conferences.

SHANNON CROUCH

After graduating from Loyola College in Maryland, Shannon Crouch was recruited by Agora Publishing, one of the largest financial newsletter publishers in the United States, to oversee the marketing efforts for The Oxford Club, one of its largest divisions.

During her tenure, she helped to successfully launch several key publications and played an integral role in improving the customer experience.

In 1999 she was recruited by Ms. Nolan and The Sovereign Society to oversee day-to-day operations and manage all publishing activities for the group. She was instrumental in creating innovative new products and services for members of the Society. In her more than nine years with The Sovereign Society, Ms. Crouch spent a considerable amount of time getting to know and understand the needs of high-net-worth individuals and their families. She too travels extensively throughout Europe, Asia, the Caribbean, and Central America, seeking out opportunities and contacts for members.

In 2007, after spending nearly 19 years in the international asset protection and investment arena, Ms. Nolan and Ms. Crouch saw a growing need to help people research and build international wealth plans and launched their newest business venture, N&C International Wealth Consultants, LLC (www.nolan-crouch.com).